Capital Walks in Edinburgh

The New Town

David Dick

Neil Wilson Publishing ● Glasgow

© David Dick, 1994

Published by Neil Wilson Publishing Ltd
309 The Pentagon Centre
36 Washington Street
GLASGOW G3 8AZ
Tel: 041-221-1117
Fax: 041-221-5363

The moral right of the author has been asserted.
A catalogue record for this book is available from the British
Library.

ISBN 1-897784-20-1

Typeset in 8.5/9pt Clarendon by Face to Face Design
Services, Glasgow

Printed in Musselburgh by Scotprint Ltd

All photographs within the publication are by the author

Contents

Acknowledgements

My thanks are overdue to Mrs Rita Reid MA (Hons) for checking much of the text. To my wife, Muriel, for typing, proof-reading and patience and for learning the intricacies of the word-processor, I owe more than simple gratitude. I am indebted to Mr Alec Barron BA (Hons), retired Dean of the Faculty of Humanities of Napier University, for his invaluable help in the presentation of these Capital Walks.

Preface

So often during our holiday to a city much of its historical significance is missed in a brief glance at its streets and statues and one is left with the thought: 'I wish I could remember more; it was such a lovely city'. As you wander the streets of Edinburgh's New Town this book will give you not only some historical facts and fables but brief historical biographies and backgrounds to the famous and the not so famous and so, hopefully, a permanent memory of your visit.

To the resident of Edinburgh, if you are as unaware of the wonders of your city as I was when I started this series of walks then you can look forward to the joy of discovering the many interesting talking points with friends and visitors.

The layout of this book is easy to follow: it is split into three sections for each capital walk with a street map detailing each location; the encircled numbers simply correspond with the numbered histories and biographies which follow so that you can go from one to the other consecutively or skip some as you wish. A series of short biographies accompanies each capital walk, and these are followed by the more detailed entries at the end of each section. Your walks can therefore be as long or as short as you wish to make them. They will also be governed by the weather, and doubtless the numerous welcoming hostelries which abound in the New Town! Essentially though, these walks are designed to take up a morning or an afternoon. Enjoy Edinburgh, it is a great city.

David Dick
January 1994

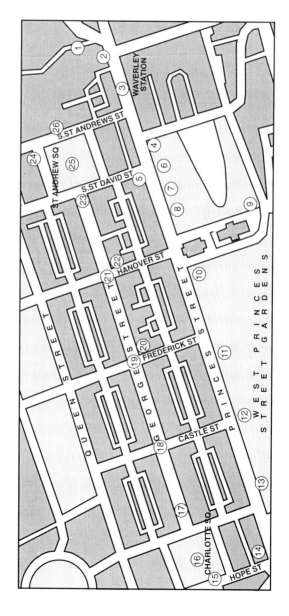

Capital Walk 1

We start at the east end of Princes Street on the corner of Register House with the St James Centre behind and Princes Street ahead, on the right-hand-side is a small lane, James Craig Walk, which leads to the bus station and New St Andrews House.

1   James Craig Walk

Named in 1972 after James Craig (1744-95) the medal-winning architect who was given the Freedom of the City of Edinburgh for his design of the New Town of Edinburgh in 1766. It was Lord Provost Drummond's dream but unfortunately he died in the year of the competition. Craig himself died before the completion of the New Town, the land being considered too exposed and some influential people were not attracted by the rectilinear layout of the streets, but it was to become the most splendid example of Georgian architecture in Britain.

2   Wellington Statue

Arthur Wellesley, the 1st Duke of Wellington (1769-1852), the famous army commander whose victory at the Battle of Waterloo in 1815 finally ended the Napoleonic Wars. He was Prime Minister in 1828 but he was not a successful politician. He opposed parliamentary reform and seemed unaware of the plight of the poor.

3   Princes Street

Named St Giles Street in Craig's original plan but George III requested that it be changed to Princes Street in honour of his two sons, the first of which was the Prince of Wales (1762-1830) who was to become Regent in 1811 and George IV in 1820. He was handsome, brilliant, charming but wildly extravagant. He hated his father and patronised 'Regency' architecture. The other Prince was Frederick, Duke of York (1763-1827), a courageous soldier but not too bright; the well known children's parody was written about him:

> *The noble Duke of York*
> *He had ten thousand men*
> *He marched them up to the top of the hill*
> *And he marched them down again*

As Commander-in-Chief of the British Army he

improved the training of officers and the well-being of the men to give him a well disciplined army.

We now cross Princes Street to the newly refurbished Balmoral Hotel (formerly the North British Hotel), past the Waverley Steps and Market (named after Sir Walter Scott's Waverley novels) and proceed along to East Princes Street Gardens.

4 David Livingstone Statue

The Scottish medical missionary (1813-73) and explorer of Africa who died trying to discover the source of the Nile. He discovered and named the Victoria Falls and spread Christianity to many remote parts of Africa. He died in the wild and his devoted African bearers carried his body hundreds of miles back to the coast.

5 Jenners

Jenners opened in 1834 as Kennington and Jenner and became simply Jenners after the death of Charles Kennington in 1862. Charles Jenner was not simply a hard working businessman, he was also a kindly philanthropist who gave unstintingly of his time and money for the benefit of the poor and the sick in Edinburgh. He set up the United Industrial School and was a founder member and director of the Royal Hospital for Sick Children. His store was destroyed in the great fire of 1892 and he commissioned William Hamilton Beattie to design the present store, insisting on the frontage as a copy of the Bodleian Library in Oxford. He died in 1893, eighteen months before the grand opening on 6th May 1895.

6 The Scott Monument

Some 200ft/61m high, this Gothic steeple by George Kemp has 287 steps to its gallery at the top and sixty-four statuette characters from the novels of Sir Walter Scott (1771-1832) whose white marble figure with his deerhound, Maida was sculpted by John Steell. Scott was born and educated in Edinburgh and practised law in his father's law firm before giving his whole attention to his literary work. He built his prestigious house, Abbotsford on the Tweed near Melrose, but the stock market crash of 1826 almost bankrupted him. He resolutely refused bankruptcy and wrote himself to death to repay his debts saying, 'I will involve no friend, rich or poor. My own right hand shall do it'.

7   Adam Black Monument

Erected in 1877 to commemorate this straightforward, forthright, honest politician (1784-1874) — a Liberal, greatly respected in Parliament and twice Lord Provost of Edinburgh between 1843 and 1848. His publishing company produced the *Edinburgh Review* of which the jurist Francis Jeffrey was editor for twenty-seven years.

8   John Wilson Statue

Commemorates a gifted Scottish journalist (1785-1854) who wrote under the pseudonym 'Christopher North' and was Professor of Moral Philosophy of the University of Edinburgh. In addition to *Lights and Shadows of Scottish Life*, *The Trials of Margaret Lyndsay* and *The Forresters*, he wrote over half of the popular *Noctes Ambrosianae*.

9   Playfair Steps, Royal Scottish Academy, National Gallery

The Playfair Steps which lead to the top of the Mound are named after William Henry Playfair (1789-1857) Edinburgh's principal architect who designed the Royal Scottish Academy, the National Gallery, Donaldson's School for the Deaf, the City Observatory on the Calton Hill, the National Memorial (unfinished) and the memorials to his uncle Professor John Playfair and Dugald Stewart.

10 Allan Ramsay Monument

Another literary figure, in Carrara marble by John Steell, erected in 1848. Allan Ramsay (1686-1758) was a Scottish poet and a man of diverse interests. He started the 'Easy Club' in 1712 for fellow intellectuals, he had a shop in Niddry Street where he sold books and he started the first lending library in the country. He designed his own house called Ramsay Lodge (nicknamed the 'goose pie'), he built a theatre in an era of Scottish Kirk disapproval of drama, he played golf and invented toys and games for his children and their friends.

11 Scots Greys Boer War Memorial

A mounted trooper in bronze by Birnie Rhind, 1906, commemorates this famous Scottish Regiment's battles in the Boer War (1899-1902) in which they were the first to wear camouflage (a lesson from the Boers) and undertook the last full cavalry charge of the British Army. The birth of the Regiment took place in the Borders; three troops were raised in 1678 and fought at Bothwell Bridge against the Covenanters. In 1704 they fought at Blenheim, captured the French Eagle at Waterloo in 1815 and won many battle honours at the Crimea, the Great War and in World War II.

12 Dr Thomas Guthrie Monument

Opposite Castle Street is a memorial of a great churchman whose unfailing devotion and concern for the poor led to his creation of the Original Schools which started from 'food, clothing and education' for seven boys to even better provision for over four hundred boys and girls within a year. His philosophy was 'Patience, Prayer and Porridge: porridge first and the other two might follow.' The inscription on his monument is a fitting epithet:

> Dr Thomas Guthrie DD 1803-73. An eloquent preacher of the gospel, founder of the Edinburgh Original Ragged Industrial Schools and by tongue and pen the apos-

tle of the movement elsewhere. One of the earliest Temperance Reformers. A friend of the poor and the oppressed.

13 Sir James Simpson Statue

This is the famous gynaecologist and obstetrician who took the excruciating pain out of surgery and made childbirth bearable. Sir James Simpson (1811-70), after whom the Simpson Maternity Pavillion is named, discovered the use of chloroform as an effective anaesthetic in 1847; it gained the seal of Royal approval in 1853 when Queen Victoria used it at the birth of Prince Leopold

14 Hope Street

Having crossed over Princes Street, Hope Street is the last street off Princes Street on the right hand side and is named after Charles Hope of Granton (1763-1851), a grandson of the 1st Earl of Hopetoun, who was appointed Lord Advocate in 1801, Lord Justice Clerk in 1804, Lord President of the Court of Session in 1811 and was Tory MP for the City of Edinburgh.

15 Charlotte Square

Designed by Robert Adam and residence to many famous names — Earl Haig, Lord Cockburn, Leander Starr Jameson, the Marquis of Bute, Alexander Graham Bell, Lord Joseph Lister, Sir Robert Philip among them. The square is named after the wife of George III, Queen Charlotte (1744-1818) who bore him fifteen children and suffered the goading criticism of her eldest son against her husband who became insane. She cared for him without help and died of overwork two years before him.

16 Prince Albert Monument

In the middle of the garden of Charlotte Square, this monument was unveiled in 1876 by his wife, Queen Victoria, fifteen years after his early death aged forty-two. She knighted the sculptor John Steell for his 30ft/9m-high equestrian figure of the Prince Consort in the uniform of a Field Marshal. Prince Albert (1819-61) was a peace-loving man who worked himself to the point of exhaustion in politics but was mistrusted by Lord Palmerston and the Whigs. He encouraged the arts, social improvements and industrial innovation. The Great Exhibition of 1851 at Crystal Palace was his all-consuming interest. He brought the Christmas tree to Britain, he pestered Parliament for sewers for London and actively supported Lord Shaftesbury to improve the terrible conditions of the poor. He brought new respect for the Royal Family, but because of his German birth he was never wholly trusted.

17 George Street

The main street according to Craig's plan is named after the monarch George III (1738-1820). He reigned for sixty years but during the last ten years he was insane. His early years as king were a disaster in government but he had a few good years with Pitt the Younger as Prime Minister. The American colonies were lost in 1776 due to his stubborn adherence to Lord North's intolerable taxation and he angrily opposed Irish emancipation. His eldest son and his political opponents ridiculed him unmercifully but when he died, aged eighty-two, blind and insane there was genuine grief expressed by the people.

18 Thomas Chalmers Statue

At the junction of George Street and Castle Street, this statue commemorates a great Churchman who led the 'Disruption' of 1843 when 470 churchmen walked out of the General Assembly of the Church of Scotland in protest against patronage. Thomas Chalmers (1780-1847) was an amazing man — an inspiring preacher, a gifted teacher — he was Assistant Professor of Chemistry and Mathematics at St Andrews University, Professor of Moral Philosophy at St Andrews, Professor of Theology at the University of Edinburgh and as a Parish Minister he raised almost one third of a million pounds (about £25 million today) to build 220 new churches. He founded the New College of the Free Church and was its first Principal and Professor of Divinity.

19 William Pitt Statue

At the intersection of Frederick Street, this statue was erected in 1833 and sculpted by Sir Francis Chantrey. William Pitt, 2nd Earl of Chatham became an MP at the age of twenty-two and in 1784, at twenty-five, was the youngest ever British Prime Minister. His ministry was to last almost twenty years and ended tragically with his early death at forty-six. He is credited with the construction of the modern British State; he steadily got rid of the worst corruption and Whig sinecures to give Parliament greater constitutional significance and more control to the people.

20 Frederick Street

Named after George III's father, Frederick Louis, Prince of Wales (1707-51) who was detested by his father, George II. He was weak, indecisive and slightly ridiculous but he was a discerning collector of works of art. He died aged forty-four, nine years before his father.

21 George IV Statue

At the junction of George Street and Hanover Street is a bronze by Sir Francis Chantrey in 1831. George IV's visit to Edinburgh in 1822 was organised by Sir Walter Scott and was the first by a reigning monarch since Charles II in 1650. It was a huge success. This was George IV at his best; he was a superb showman and insisted on drinking only illicit Glenlivet malt whisky rather than inferior legal produce! His extravagant and dissipated life ended tragically in a reclusive fantasy world at Windsor. His influence on architecture, furniture and sartorial elegance was quite splendid.

22 Hanover Street

Commemorates the Royal House of Hanover which started with George I in 1714 and continued until the reign of Queen Victoria in 1837. There were six Hanoverian sovereigns: George I (1714-27), George II (1727-60), George III (1760-1820), George IV (1820-30), William IV (1830-37), Queen Victoria (1837-1901). She was excluded from the Hanoverian throne — only males could accede to the crown of Hanover.

23 North & South St David Street

Named after the Patron Saint of Wales, St David (c520-589AD). His early life was spent on a Welsh island studying the scriptures. At Glastonbury he experienced hard labour and dedicated himself to helping the poor. He was an inspiring preacher and became Primate of Wales. The cult of St David was approved by Pope Callistus II in 1120. He travelled widely to establish over fifty monasteries and advocated absolute silence, rigorous fasting and total abstinence in Welsh monastic life.

24 Saint Andrew Square

Commemorates the patron saint of Scotland who was crucified on a diagonal cross. He was one of the twelve apostles and brought his brother, Simon Peter, to meet Christ. His cross on a blue background was adopted as the national emblem in 735AD after a vision appeared to the King of the Picts at the Battle of Athelstaneford. Two relics of St Andrew are contained in St Andrew's Metropolitan Cathedral in York Place.

25 Melville Monument

Standing in the central garden of Saint Andrew Square, this monument was erected by Naval officers and men in 1921. Henry Dundas, 1st Viscount Melville (1742-1811) was a despot and absolute dictator who virtually managed the affairs of Scotland as 'King Harry the ninth' as he was nicknamed. He was Lord President of the Court of Session as was his grandfather and great-grandfather before him. Using his immense influence and a great deal of bribery he 'delivered' three-quarters of the parliamentary seats of Scotland to his Prime Minister William Pitt in 1790. As Treasurer of the Navy he was alleged to have borrowed money from Navy funds; his impeachment and trial which found him innocent of any fraud effectively ended the Dundas-Pitt era.

26 Earl of Hopetoun Monument, 36 St Andrew Square

In the garden of No.36 St Andrew Square is a bronze, by sculptor Thomas Campbell, of Sir John Hope, 4th Earl of Hopetoun (1765-1823). He was a brave soldier under Sir Ralph Abercrombie and a heroic general under the Duke of Wellington. He served in the West Indies, Spain, Portugal and France. He was a governor of the Royal Bank of Scotland and well respected in both army and civilian life.

Appropriately this tour walk ends inside this magnificent Georgian house, designed by Sir William Chambers for Sir Laurence Dundas in 1772-74, which is the registered office of the Royal Bank of Scotland. The banking hall was added in 1858 with its 120-starred dome. Inlaid on the floor of the entrance hall there is a small brass plate which denotes the datum point of James Craig's rectangular system of streets in his New Town plan.

Historical Biographies

1   James Craig Walk

At the east end of Princes Street adjacent to the St James Centre is a narrow lane which leads to New St Andrews House; this is James Craig Walk, and is your starting point.

Who was James Craig? He was a relatively unknown young architect who, in 1766, was chosen by John Adam, Lord Kaimes and several other eminent men including the Lord Provost Gilbert Lawrie, as the winner of the gold medal competition for the design of the New Town.

Lord Provost George Drummond (1687-1766), six times Lord Provost of Edinburgh, had worked assiduously for the creation of the New Town and in the year of his death the Town Council advertised for the submission of designs. Craig won the coveted gold medal and was given the Freedom of the City. After his plan was redrawn in consultation with John Adam it was finally submitted in July 1767 to the king with the words:

> To His Sacred Majesty George III. The munificent Patron of every polite and liberal art. This plan of the new streets and squares, intended for his ancient Capital of the North of Britain; one of the happy consequences of the peace, security and liberty his people enjoy under his auspicious Government. Is, with the utmost Humility Inscribed by His Majesty's most devoted servant and subject James Craig.

His design was attractive because of its simplicity — a rectangular grid system of streets; its datum point is represented by a small brass circular plate inlaid on the floor of the entrance hall of the Georgian house at No.36 Saint Andrew Square which is the registered office of the Royal Bank of Scotland and at which point this tour walk will end. This magnificent house was originally built for Sir Laurence Dundas of Kerse from 1772 to 1774.

James Craig was born in 1744. His father, William Craig, was a successful Edinburgh merchant and his mother, Mary, was the youngest daughter of the Reverend Thomas Thomson of Ednan in Roxburghshire. Her brother was the poet who wrote *The Seasons*, a completely new style of poetry for the age.

Young James Craig was a pupil of Sir Robert Taylor and before his medal-winning design of the New Town he had designed the tenements of St James Square (sadly demolished in 1965 to make way for the incongruous St James Centre) and Merchant Street, a sought-after address until George IV Bridge was built over it. In addition he designed Physicians' Hall (1775) which was demolished for David Rhind's huge porticoed Commercial Bank, now the Royal Bank of Scotland at No.14 George Street. He designed Observatory House with its Gothic tower on Calton Hill for Thomas Short, an optician-astronomer, with advice from Robert Adam. Building actually started in 1776 but lack of money caused a delay and the building was finished 16 years later.

It took many years to sell the feus in the New Town; various reasons were given — the land was considered to be too exposed and some influential people were not attracted by the rectilinear layout of the streets. Craig died aged 51 in 1795, disappointed that he had not lived to see the complete plan of his New Town to fruition.

Some designs by James Craig: St James's Square, 1773; Merchant Street, 1774; North corner block of Candlemaker Row; New Town, 1776; Physicians' Hall, George Street, 1775 — demolished in 1843 to make way for David Rhind's Royal Bank of Scotland; Nos.37-38 St Andrew Square, 1781; Leith Fort entrance.

2 *Wellington Statue*

Only a few yards from James Craig Walk and immediately in front of Register House is the statue of 1848, by John Steell, of Wellington on his horse Copenhagen. It is unusual because it is supported by its hind legs and tail — a difficult problem of casting and setting up by James Gowans in 1852.

The statue, as well as Wellington Place in Leith and Wellington Street off Hillside Crescent, is named after Arthur Wellesley, 1st Duke of Wellington. Appropriately, his statue is facing the North Bridge and he, looking towards and pointing to Waterloo Place, reminds us of his great victory — the Battle of Waterloo, on 18th June 1815 when he routed the French after Napoleon's escape from the island of Elba.

Arthur Wellesley was born three months before Napoleon on 1st May 1769, fourth son of the 1st Earl of Mornington. He took his studies in military strategy very seriously and his brother, Richard, who became Baron Wellesley and Governor General of India, purchased for him the command of the 33rd Foot (the practice of buying military rank was not uncommon in those days). Arthur more than justified his brother's generosity especially during his eight years in India where his successful campaigns earned him a KCB (Knight Commander of the Most Honourable Order of the Bath), giving him the title Sir Arthur and a sword of honour from the inhabitants of Calcutta.

He was elected MP for Rye in 1806 and appointed Irish Secretary in 1807. He fought with the Spanish against Napoleon in 1808 to drive the French out of Spain to end the Peninsular War in 1814. He was awarded the GCB (Knight Grand Cross of the Most Honourable Order of the Bath) and made Field Marshal, the Duke of Wellington, KG (Knight of the Most Noble Order of the Garter), Duke of Ciudad Rodrigo, Magnate of Portugal and Parliament awarded him £400,000.

Napoleon invaded France to win four battles in

four days but in March 1814 Paris capitulated and Napoleon retreated to Fontainebleau; he was offered a truce but instead he abdicated to the 'gilded cage' of Elba where he planned his final assault. He landed in the south of France on 1st March 1815. Wellington was given only 20,000 men, the American War having weakened the British army. With the Prussians he had a total force of 67,000 to Napoleon's 74,000. Napoleon defeated Field Marshal Blücher at Ligny but his mistake was in believing that the Prussians had finally been defeated. Instead Blücher joined Wellington and attacked the French on their right and at their rear. The British were almost overwhelmed but at sunset Wellington advanced and within an hour he had routed the French. Napoleon fled to Paris and abdicated in favour of his son. He was banished to St Helena where he died six years later. Wellington was hailed a hero and the greatest general of the age.

In politics Wellington supported the 'establishment' — he helped Prime Minister Peel to reorganise the Metropolitan Police and he became Prime Minister in 1828 but his ministry was a failure. However his high reputation and eminence helped to curb the excesses of George IV and to restrain the hated Duke of Cumberland. He seemed oblivious of the disastrous effects of the Corn Laws, the Poor Laws, the troubles in agriculture and the labour revolt. The windows of his home at Apsley House were smashed on the anniversary of the Battle of Waterloo. There was confusion in Parliament with cries for reform; the ensuing election brought in many reformers and Wellington resigned.

In 1834 Earl Grey, the champion of the Reform Bill, retired and Wellington again formed a government. He was chosen as Chancellor of Oxford University and he joined the Peel Cabinet of 1841. He had now served under four sovereigns: George III, George IV, William IV and Queen Victoria. He retired from politics aged seventy-seven and in 1848 he organised the army to contain the Chartists who had assembled on Kennington Common to march on Parliament. His final retirement to Walmer Castle as Lord Warden of the Cinque Ports was the place of his peaceful death on 14th September 1852 aged eighty-three. He was buried with national honours in St Paul's Cathedral.

3   *Princes Street*

Princes Street was purposely laid out with buildings on one side to preserve the magnificent view of its gardens and Edinburgh Castle. Sir William Forbes (1739-1806), the Scottish banker, took out a Bill of Suspension and Interdict to ensure that the stretch between Waverley Bridge and Hanover Street should become a garden. Beyond Hanover Street, to the west, feus were applied for but thankfully never granted; the 1816 Act of Parliament made it illegal to build on the south side after that year.

In James Craig's plan George Street, named after George III, was the main street with more prestigious houses than in Princes Street or Queen Street. Because of its open view to the south, Princes Street became the most attractive and towards the end of the nineteenth century several large shops and hotels appeared. For example, the Royal British Hotel, by J. MacIntyre Henry in 1896-8, the R.W.Forsyth Edwardian department store (now a consortium of shops) by John J. Burnet in 1906, the first to be built using steel frame construction; the Old Waverley Hotel by John Armstrong in 1883 and Jenners, the biggest department store in Britain in its day (see Capital Walk 1, number 5 on page 31); it was designed by William Hamilton Beattie in 1893-95. This Renaissance pink stone edifice has a splayed corner copied from the Bodleian Library in Oxford.

In James Craig's original design of the New Town (1776), Princes Street was named St Giles Street but when George III was consulted he felt that the name St Giles might be associated with a rather shabby area of the same name in London where muggings, vandalism and drunkenness were commonplace and the king requested that the name be changed to Princes Street after the two Royal Princes, their Royal Highnesses, the four-year-old Duke of Rothesay, the Prince of Wales and three-year-old Duke of York, Prince Frederick. It is doubtful if George III would have chosen the name in their honour had he known how critical of him they would become.

The eldest son, the Prince of Wales was born in 1762. His upbringing was strict and, whereas his father had simple tastes, he rebelled with extravagances through his gambling, his love affairs and drunkenness. He did everything he could to spite his father: he married a Roman Catholic, Mrs Fitzherbert, secretly and without his father's consent in 1785. The marriage was invalid under the Royal Marriage Act but he denied it in any case. He chose the political association of the Whigs and those statesmen whom his father detested — Fox, Burke and Sheridan. The King's insanity reached maniacal proportions in 1788 when he attacked the Prince of Wales, but he recovered and denied the Prince his desperation to reign; he had to wait another twelve years.

His lifestyle accrued huge debts totalling £650,000 (almost £100 million today) which Parliament agreed to settle on condition that he settled down and married Princess Caroline, daughter of the Duke of Brunswick. He drank himself into a stupor for the marriage ceremony in 1795. Soon after the birth of their only daughter, Charlotte, his wife left him but she returned to claim the title of Queen in 1820 when he became King. She was never recognised as Queen and was refused entry to Westminster Hall at the coronation. He tried to divorce her by accusing her of adultery while he lived a life of licentiousness. He forced the introduction of a Bill in Parliament to deprive her of the title 'Queen' and to declare her marriage 'forever wholly dissolved, annulled and made void.' A London mob threatened to riot in support of her, shouting 'No Queen, No King!' and George cleared out for safety's sake; at one point his life was threatened with assassination. However, she died on 7th August 1821.

The year after his accession he visited Ireland and Hanover and in 1822 his visit to Scotland, in grand style, was organised by Sir Walter Scott. This was a great success, he paraded along Princes Street wearing the Stuart tartan and the people loved it. Many Edinburgh streets were named after him — George IV Bridge, Regent Bridge, Gardens, Lane, Place, Road, Street, Street Lane, Terrace and Terrace Lane, Rothesay Place and Terrace, Royal Crescent and Terrace, Carlton Terrace, Terrace Lane and Mews, Chester Street, Cornwall Street, King's Bridge Road and Place, Windsor Terrace, Place and Street.

Towards the end of his life he lived in an almost fantasy world; he even pretended to have played a major part in winning the Battle of Waterloo but whether this was to annoy the ageing Duke of Wellington or whether he was going mad, no-one quite knew. He lived as a recluse at Windsor and died aged sixty-eight on 26th June 1830. His life was a poor example to his subjects but at his best his wit was scintillatingly brilliant, his conversation sparkled, his dress elegant and his influence upon architecture, furniture and dress was quite splendid. Nevertheless, he died a sorry figure. (A more comprehensive biography of George IV appears in Capital Walk 1, number 21 on page 74).

The other Prince of Princes Street was Frederick the Duke of York, George III's second son (there were nine sons and six daughters) whose Scottish title is the Duke of Albany, from which Albany Street is named; York Place takes its name from his English title.

Frederick was born in 1763 and although he was educated in England he was trained for a military career in Germany as was the custom with Hanoverian Royalty. Aged twenty-eight he married Frederica, Princess Royal of Prussia. This was a period of revolution and Europe was in turmoil. The Bastille had been taken in July 1789, the Belgians revolted, Louis XVI fled from Paris in July 1791 and France declared war offering aid to all freedom-seeking peoples. Following the execution of Louis XVI, the Duke of York, in commamd of an army against the revolutionary forces, was initially successful in Flanders when he captured Valence and was hailed 'King of France' but his euphoria was short-lived — he was badly defeated at Dunkirk and at Flanders in Belgium. By 1794 he had been driven back to Hanover but he could not be faulted for lack of courage and energy. His siege of Valenciennes was successful but was not followed up and his campaign collapsed. The acrimony in Parliament threatened Pitt and he withdrew the command from the Duke who was the subject of the children's parody:

> *The noble Duke of York*
> *He had ten thousand men*
> *He marched them up to the top of the hill*
> *And he marched them down again.*

As Commander-in-Chief of the British Army in 1798 he set about improving discipline by examining the root cause of the malaise which had beset it. The system of recruiting was disorganised and considered unfair by the regular soldiers who, being enlisted for life, found themselves poorer than the short-term militia men. The Duke's first step was to improve the status and pay of the regulars; he then started the Staff College to formalise the training of officers. He therefore deserves credit for giving Wellington disciplined, efficient and well-trained officers with whom he defeated the French at Waterloo. Wellington, however was less than pleased since the Duke had appointed staff officers without consulting him.

In 1799, Bonaparte's offer of peace was refused and the Duke, again in command of the British Army, made a disastrous attempt to link up with the Russian Army; Wellington was to say of it, 'at least I learned what not to do.'

The Duke's personal 'affairs of the heart' caught up with him; he had discarded one mistress too many; Mrs Mary Ann Clarke, encouraged by some radicals, was coerced to give evidence against the Duke in relation to the sale of army commissions. However he was exonerated and Mrs Clarke was imprisoned for libel having gone too far in her accusations by implicating the Duke of Wellington. The Duke of York's reputation was such that his effigy was burned in Suffolk and in Yorkshire; he resigned his office but was reinstated in 1811. He died in 1827 with no family, his memory smeared by scandal.

4   David Livingstone Statue

Crossing over Princes Street to the newly refurbished Balmoral Hotel and passing the Waverley Market, the first statue in Princes Street Gardens is that of David Livingstone. Some think of Livingstone as a great healer of native Africans, whom he loved and many of whom he saved from slavery. Others think of him as a great discoverer — the first to set eyes on the great Lake Ngami (which disappeared, evaporating to a flat plain). He recharted the Zambesi River, in the process of which he discovered the 5700 ft/ 1737m wide waterfall which he named Victoria Falls in honour of the monarch and he died in his search for the source of the Nile. And others still, will think of him as a devoted missionary who brought Christianity to remote parts of Africa whose people responded because his religion was practical and healing. In fact he was all three: doctor, missionary and explorer.

David Livingstone was born in 1813 and brought up in a one-roomed house in Low Blantyre, Lanarkshire. He had a thirst for knowledge; even while working from the age of ten years as a spinner in a cotton factory, he found time to study. In the Scottish tradition, he loved study for its own sake and went on to the University of Glasgow to take degrees in both Medicine and Theology and, being so well qualified, he was accepted for training as a Missionary by the London Missionary Society in 1838. Not exactly a paragon of sartorial excellence, in fact he was positively scruffy and a hopeless orator, he almost failed in his training period; but what was very obvious was his sparkling intelligence and sheer integrity of character. These ensured his success and so in December 1840, influenced by Dr Robert Moffat, he went to Africa (rather than China — his first preference) where missionaries were badly needed.

He was not content with well established missions: he explored the unknown, always slowly, because his prime purpose was that of healing the sick and converting the savages to the Christian faith. He had an enforced sabbatical having been savaged by a lion and during his year-long convalescence at Kuruman he was nursed by Mary Moffat, daughter of his mentor, the missionary Dr Robert Moffat. They were married in 1844, he, aged thirty-one and she, twenty-three. Mary was devoted to him and his work; she accompanied him into the unknown to suffer unbelievable hardships. As is often the case with dedicated men, Livingstone seemed unaware of his young wife's sufferings even during her pregnancies in the wild. She only just made it back to relative civilization while pregnant with their fourth child which sadly died. She was so weak she had to return home to Britain in 1852.

Livingstone pressed on to even greater discoveries and greater fame. He took full charge of his next expedition but his lack of planning and management skill was a major handicap and he had to return. His wife had died in 1862 while trapped on board a ship in the inhospitable Zambesi River. His grief seemed to strengthen his resolve to discover Lake Nyasa, to continue to help the sick and to halt the slave trade of the Portuguese. In Malawi (formerly Nyasaland) the town of Blantyre was named in honour of Livingstone's birthplace and Livingstonia in northern Zambia is named after him.

After about a year at home he set out again to Africa to discover the source of the Nile. For the next five years he was lost to the world and Henry Morton Stanley, sent by the *New York Herald*, found Livingstone in Ujiji after a long and seemingly hopeless search, introducing himself with the famous words: 'Dr Livingstone, I presume.' Livingstone was by then seriously ill, being emaciated and badly in need of fresh supplies and medical attention. The welcome visitors stayed for several months and tried to persuade Livingstone to return with them but he insisted on pursuing his goal and died in the attempt in April 1873.

He was sixty years old. His devoted African bearers travelled several hundred miles to bring his body back to his own people on the coast. There was national mourning and he lies buried in Westminster Abbey, London.

5 Jenners

Jenners of Princes Street has been synonymous with high quality shopping in Edinburgh for almost 160 years. The shop was opened as Kennington and Jenner on 1st May 1834 at No.47 Princes Street by two young men, Charles Kennington and Charles Jenner, who had recently learned a salutary lesson from their employer, a draper in Leith Street. They had been given a 'hot tip' for the Musselburgh races and had asked their employer for the day off work. He had refused them bluntly, but ignoring him, they took their day at the races. On returning to work next day they found themselves without a job. They had been summarily dismissed.

It is probable that their winnings financed their decision to open a shop of their own. They had each received a sound training in the drapery business and they leased two shops from a tobacco manufacturer in Princes Street. Soon the ladies of Edinburgh found not only attractive clothes and accessories but good service with added charm. The young men prospered and by 1860 they had extended their shop through the purchase of No.48 Princes Street and Nos.2,4,6&8 South St David Street. But tragedy struck; Charles Kennington died in 1862. The two men had formed a perfect partnership. Charles Jenner felt the loss deeply but his staff depended on him to carry on. There were now almost fifty employees and the demand for their goods was increasing. Charles Jenner threw himself into even harder work, not only for the business, which continued to grow, but in work for the poor. By 1875 it was necessary to add four storeys to the Princes Street building which was now called simply Jenners and was the biggest retailer in Scotland.

Charles Jenner had not confined his considerable energy and business acumen to his business alone; his contributions to charities were generous. He did not

31

give money merely to salve his conscience, he gave unstintingly of his time to work with the poor and the sick. The state of society in his time was cause for deep concern: in 1850 almost 5000 children were 'challenged for begging' and 46 were convicted of crimes (mostly theft); the mortality rate in the first five years of life was over 40% in the Old Town and 18% in the New Town.

Jenner gave of his time and money to set up the United Industrial School in Blackfriars Street. Thomas Guthrie (1803-73) had published his first *Plea for Ragged Schools* in 1847 and Jenner was undoubtedly affected by this good minister's magnificent example. Guthrie had started his first Original School in a room at Ramsay Garden and within a year he had increased its roll from seven boys to over 400 boys and girls. Jenner became chairman of the School Board of the United Industrial School. In 1860 the mortality rate of babies was so worrying to him he set about the establishment of the Royal Hospital for Sick Children at Meadowside House becoming a founder member and director. Within a short time it was obvious that larger premises were required and Jenner made the largest single contribution for a new hospital at Sciennes Road on the site of the Trades Maidens' Hospital. He was chairman of the directors in 1869.

After forty-three years of extremely dedicated work and service to the community Charles Jenner decided to retire to his beautiful home, Easter Duddingston Lodge with its magnificent gardens. He had leased the Lodge and its land from the Duke of Abercorn in 1858 and had spent sixteen years in its improvement. In 1874 the Duke decided to dispose of it and Jenner made an offer which was accepted. He immediately set about an extensive reconstruction to the plan of William Hamilton Beattie (1840-98). He then purchased adjoining land to give him a garden of eight and a half acres. This was to become his all-consuming hobby in retirement.

However tragedy struck again; the wonderful store, to which he had given a lifetime of work, was completely destroyed in the great fire of 1892. The damage was estimated to be £250,000 and 120 employees who lived on the premises suddenly found themselves in the street with nothing but the clothes they wore. Jenner saw to it that they were given temporary living accommodation in Craiglockhart Hydro (now part of Napier University). As far as the people of Edinburgh were concerned this was a civic calamity and the Town Council responded with an offer of temporary premises. In the event, legal problems arose and the offer had to be withdrawn. Charles Jenner found the solution himself. He came out of retirement to organise the adaptation of the Rose Street premises as a temporary shop. Jenners was in business again and after five weeks every employee was back at work.

Jenner then set about the planning of a new building on the existing site and he again asked the eminent architect William Hamilton Beattie to accept a commission to design the new building. Jenner had visited the Bodleian Library in Oxford and he convinced Beattie to base his design of the new Jenners on this magnificent building. The final result astonished and delighted the 25,000 citizens of Edinburgh who arrived on its opening day — 6th May 1895. It was modern in every respect with extensive electric lighting, air conditioning and fast lifts — all innovations of their time. Sadly Charles Jenner did not live to see the grand opening; he had died on 27th October 1893 but this magnificent building was a grand memorial to this hard-working and generous man.

6 *The Scott Monument*

The 200ft/61m high Scott Monument with its 287 steps to the gallery at the top dominates the Princes Street skyline. The white marble figure of Sir Walter, by John Steell, sits with his beloved deerhound Maida at the base. The monument, a Gothic steeple by George Meikle Kemp, was completed in 1846 at a cost of £15,650. Scott never imagined for a moment that the Galashiels millwright to whom he gave a lift in his carriage would some day build his monument with its sixty-four statuette characters from his novels, sixteen Scottish poets and three kings set into niches around it.

It is often said that Sir Walter wrote himself to death to repay debts of £117,000 following the panic on the London money market in 1826. Scott was an honourable man. He refused the option of bankruptcy and offers of help from his friends, instead he took on the enormous task of writing his way out of his debts saying, 'I will involve no friend, rich or poor. My own right hand shall do it.'

Walter Scott was born on 15th August 1771 in College Wynd (now Guthrie Street); his father loved the old place but he felt compelled to move having lost six children in infancy. Walter, the ninth of twelve children, probably owes his survival from the fact that he was sent, aged two years, to his grandfather at Sandyknowe near Kelso, but he contracted infantile paralysis, and thus a limp throughout his life. He spent his lonely days reading; one ballad in particular caught his imagination — *Hardyknute, a Fragment* which had been reprinted by Allan Ramsay in his *Evergreen* — Scott learned the 216-line ballad by heart.

In 1772 the Scott family took up residence at No.25 George Square. Young Walter must have been enormously influenced by his father, a strict Calvinist, who was a respected Edinburgh solicitor. One of his clients,

John Murray, the secretary to Prince Charles Edward Stuart, was given the courtesy of a cup of tea by Mrs Scott and when he left Walter's father threw the cup and saucer out of the window. Murray had been captured at the Battle of Culloden and had betrayed some of the Prince's men. No member of the Scott family would again drink from that tainted cup!

From George Square the Scott family filled their pew in Greyfriars Church every Sunday. It was in this historical church that Walter fell in love for the first time; the object of his adoration was Miss Williamina Stuart; he shyly offered her his umbrella and escorted her home. He was broken-hearted when she married the banker Sir William Forbes who became a friend of Scott and is remembered for taking out a Bill of Suspension and Interdict in 1771 to prevent any building on the south side of Princes Street.

In 1786 Scott was apprenticed in his father's law firm and after his studies at the University of Edinburgh he was called to the bar in 1792. Five years later he married a French lady, Charlotte Charpentier. Their first house was at No.10 South Castle Street then to No.2 and finally to No.39 where they lived for the next twenty-four years. Their summer house was Hawthornden in Lasswade. He was appointed Sheriff of Selkirkshire in 1799 with a salary of £300 a year to which he added another £1300 when he became Clerk of the Sessions and he expected to earn a further £1000 a year from his writing.

Scott's first published work was *The Minstrelsy of the Scottish Border* in two volumes in 1802 which was followed by the poem *The Lay of the Last Minstrel* in 1805. It was about this time that Scott decided to make his career a literary one, although it was his ambition ultimately to become a Scottish laird. After he moved from his summer house in Lasswade to Ashestiel on the Tweed he wrote *Marmion, The Life of Dryden* and *The Lady of the Lake* — his most popular narrative poem.

Scott built his prestigious house, Abbotsford, on the Tweed in 1812 and from then on his literary output was prodigious — *Rakeby, The Life and Work of Swift, Waverley, The Black Dwarf, Old Mortality, The Heart of Midlothian* (written in the garden of Duddingston House), *The Legend of Montrose* and *Ivanhoe* — all written between 1813 and 1819. He wrote anonymously and had become so popular that he was called 'The Great Un-known' but he acknowledged the provenance of the *Waverley Novels* after the famous comic actor, Charles Mackay, portrayed Bailie Nicol Jarvie from *Rob Roy* — Scott was ecstatic about Mackay's performances.

In 1817 Scott gained Royal permission to open the chest held in the vaults of Edinburgh Castle to 'dis-cover' the Scottish Regalia — the crown jewels of Scot-land, hidden firstly from Cromwell at Dunnottar and then in Edinburgh Castle after the Act of Union of 1707. In 1822 Scott masterminded the arrangements for the visit of George IV to Edinburgh and he personally wel-comed His Majesty aboard the Royal George at Leith when he presented the King with a silver cross of St Andrew from the ladies of Edinburgh. During the visit he took the opportunity to point to the vacant space on the King's bastion in the Castle and begged the king for the return of the giant cannon, Mons Meg.

By 1824 he had published *The Monastery*, its more successful sequel *The Abbot*, then *Kenilworth*, *The Pirate*, *The Fortunes of Nigel*, *Quentin Durward* and *Red Gauntlet*. Scott has been described as the 'saddest of authors' but he wrote objectively and is credited with the creation of the historical novel.

Scott's health was failing by 1831 and in July 1832, when sailing from London to Newhaven on the steam-ship James Watt, the captain noticed Scott's condition and gave him his cabin. He was unconscious when he landed at Newhaven but after two days rest at the King's Hotel in Saint Andrew Square he made the journey to Abbotsford. He lived only three more months. His last wish was to be taken from his bed to his favourite win-dow overlooking the Tweed; he died peacefully with his daughter by his side while he watched the glisten-ing Tweed on 21st September 1832. He was sixty-one years old. With his 'own right hand' he had written more than had several generations before him. And so ended Edinburgh's 'Golden Age'.

7 *Adam Black Monument*

Continuing along Princes Street, through the Gardens, is the monument to Adam Black, a bronze by John Hutchison, erected in 1877 to commemorate this straightforward, forthright politician— a Liberal, greatly respected in Parliament and twice Lord Provost of Edinburgh between 1843 and 1848.

Adam Black was best known in Edinburgh through his publishing company Adam Black & Son and the famous *Edinburgh Review* started with Sydney Smith, Francis Horner and several others in 1802 when Constable & Co. was the chosen publisher. Francis Jeffrey, the famous Scottish jurist, was its editor for twenty-seven years. Black and Jeffrey were born almost next door to each other in Charles Street; Black in 1784 and Jeffrey eleven years before.

Black learned the book trade in Edinburgh and in London having left the University without taking a degree. His name as a leading publisher was made when he bought the *Encyclopaedia Britannica* in 1827 after the stock market crisis of 1826 and the failure of Constable & Co. After the death of Robert Cadell (originally a partner of Archibald Constable) Black bought the novels by Walter Scott for £27,000 in 1851 to lead to further financial success of his publishing firm.

Black took a powerful stance in politics; he was City Treasurer at a time of severe financial difficulty, the City was in danger of bankruptcy and Black's astute negotiations with the creditors saved the situation. He was twice elected Lord Provost and during his second term of office he created a stir when he declined the offer of a knighthood (the only other Lord Provost to do so being Jack Kane in 1974).

He was intensely concerned for poor youngsters and strongly supported the work of the Ragged Schools started by the Rev Thomas Guthrie DD. At that time the population of the Old Town was roughly equal to that of the New Town but the mortality rate of children between ages one and five years was 40% in the Old Town and 18% in the New Town. Black insisted that this appalling mortality rate was in part due to cramped, damp and insanitary conditions and he pressed, at every opportunity, for access by ordinary people to the open spaces of the countryside and is credited as the forerunner of the Scottish Rights of Way Society. Black's voice was the dominant liberal one in the Town Council over the dissention brought about by the 'disruption' in 1843 when Thomas Chalmers led 470 churchmen out of the General Assembly of the Church of Scotland to form the Free Church.

In 1854, at the age of seventy, Black was elected Member of Parliament for the Burgh in place of Lord MacAuley who had been elevated to the peerage. In Parliament he was an independent whose strong voice lent support to free trade, the removal of sectarianism in education and total toleration in religion. He held the seat for two general elections and was defeated in 1865, at age eighty-one, by Duncan McLaren. He died aged ninety on 24th January 1874.

8 John Wilson Statue

Walking westwards along Princes Street the final statue in East Princes Street Gardens is that of Professor John Wilson, created by sculptor Sir John Steell. John Wilson held the senior chair of the University of Edinburgh, that of Moral Philosophy in 1820 and wrote under the pseudonym "Christopher North". Born at Paisley in 1785 his contemporaries and associates were poet Samuel Coleridge, writer Thomas De Quincey, poets Robert Southey and William Wordsworth when, in 1807, Wilson lived at his beloved Elleray with its magnificent view of Lake Windermere. Not only was Wilson intellectually gifted but he was well known for his athletic prowess. In 1811 he decided to give all his energies to poetry and published his *Isle of Palms* and *The City of Plague.*

He lost his inheritance in 1815 through his uncle's financial trickery; this forced him to give up his idyllic Elleray. His financial loss was Edinburgh's intellectual gain through the new publication of *Blackwood's Magazine* when, in 1817, he and John Gibson Lockhart, the scourge of the Whigs, were its mainstay. After Lockhart left for London Wilson became its unofficial editor. Lord Cockburn, in his *Memorials* wrote of their *Noctes Ambrosianae* — a series of scenes supposed to have occurred in a tavern in West Register Street:

> No periodical publication that I know of can boast so extraordinary a series of jovial dramatic fiction. Wilson, I believe, now professes to regret and condemn many things in these papers, and to deny his authorship of them; but substantially they are all his. I have not the slightest doubt that he wrote at least ninety per cent of them. I

wish no man had anything worse to be timid about … Wilson's propensity was for jovial fun and eloquence; Lockhart's for quiet bitter sarcasm. They both wrote with great spirit … and neither was troubled with delicacy — a perfect combination for a libellous periodical work.

Wilson's election to the Chair of Moral Philosophy of the University of Edinburgh in 1820 saw a continued outpouring of his genius in *Blackwood's Magazine* plus *Lights and Shadows of Scottish Life*, *The Trials of Margaret Lyndsay*, *The Foresters* and many others. His works were swallowed up by an admiring, devoted and growing public. His death in 1854 aged sixty-nine seemed unimaginable to his devotees.

*THE FACADE OF THE ROYAL SCOTTISH ACADEMY, DESIGNED BY
WILLIAM H. PLAYFAIR*

9 Playfair Steps, Royal Scottish Academy, National Gallery

Leaving East Princes Street Gardens and crossing to the Royal Scottish Academy, the distant steps to the left which lead to the top of the Mound are called the Playfair Steps and are named after William Henry Playfair who designed the Royal Scottish Academy and the National Gallery at the Mound. The Cockburn Society requested a change of name from John Knox Way to Playfair Steps in 1978.

The Royal Scottish Academy with its sixteen columns was built in 1822-26 and enlarged by Playfair in 1831. Another rank of columns with its north pediment were added to take the statue of Queen Victoria by John Steell in 1844; the total cost being about £40,000. The National Gallery, also by Playfair, was designed in 1848 and received a Treasury grant of £30,000 to add to the £20,000 raised by the Board of Manufacturers.

William H. Playfair was born in London in 1789 where his father was a reputable architect. The Playfairs were an illustrious family, William's uncle being Professor John Playfair the famous mathematician (he invented the graph) and supporter of James Hutton (the father of geology). On the death of his father William came to Edinburgh to live with his uncle.

William was trained in Edinburgh by William Stark who died in 1813. Playfair returned to London to work with the firm of Smirke and Wyatt and, after touring in France, his return to Edinburgh coincided with the competition for the design of the University of Edinburgh which had been started in 1774 by Robert Adam who died shortly before the outbreak of war with France in 1793. Playfair was selected by the Commissioners of George III and the design of the Old Quad in South Bridge is credited to him rather than to Adam.

William H. Playfair thus became Edinburgh's principal architect. One of his early designs, as resident architect under C.R.Cockerell, was the unfinished National Monument on Calton Hill to the Scots who gave their lives in the Napoleonic Wars. It was to have been a reproduction of the Parthenon in Athens but the public subscription for its completion was only sufficient for its twelve pillars. It was dubbed 'Edinburgh's Disgrace'; in fact the citizens of the capital had given generously, the rest of Scotland not being sufficiently interested in so lavish a memorial and, of course, times were hard in the 1820's after a costly war. Playfair wrote to Cockerell on 30th June 1829, 'Our Parthenon is come to a dead halt, and is, I am afraid, likely to stand up a striking proof of the pride and poverty of us Scots … Wallace's contract is finished, and what is to be done next I know not. I suppose, Nothing!'

In 1818 he designed the City Observatory in the shape of a domed Greek Cross on the Calton Hill for the Astronomical Institution, the president of which was his uncle, Professor Playfair. His monument and that to Dugald Stewart in classical Greek style were also designed by Playfair.

His 'Calton Scheme' was a masterpiece of elegance; had it been completed it might have outshone even the New Town. His plan, based on that of his teacher, William Stark, was accepted and took advantage of the hilly site; its splendid terraces overlooking their gardens — Royal Terrace to the south with Royal Terrace Gardens, Regent Terrace (1825) to the north linked by Carlton Terrace (1821). Hillside Crescent, started in 1825, with its garden was halted for thirty years due to geological difficulties. Blenheim Place (1821) and Leopold Place (1820) were all Playfair's designs. Then came the streets which radiate from Hillside Crescent: Windsor Street (1822) and Brunswick Street (1824); the others — Hillside Street and Wellington Street differ from Playfair's design having bay-windowed, four storey tenements by Thomas Beattie.

Playfair's most majestic design was Donaldson's School for the Deaf at West Coates, in 1841, which was endowed by the Edinburgh bookseller, James Donaldson, who left £220,000 for it. Queen Victoria admired it as superior to any Royal residence. Donaldson's School was his longest project taking ten years to complete due to delays in the supply of stone and difficulties with the main contractor, Young & Trench. In any case, Playfair was busy with the design of the enlargement of Floors Castle for the newly married 6th Duke of Roxburghe. His design of St Stephen's Church was made difficult by the steep slope of St Vincent Street; its 162ft/49m high clock tower has the longest pendulum in Europe. Its imposing entrance with its curved steps faces up St Vincent Street to the south and was built in 1827-28 for £18,975.

One of his last designs in 1850 was that of the National Gallery. Playfair, a conscientiously fastidious man, completed his designs in a standing position and he worked a twelve-hour day. Eventually, in middle life, he became increasingly paralysed and he died in 1857 aged sixty-eight and was buried in Dean Cemetery. In his own words: 'Nothing good in architecture can be effected without a monstrous expenditure of patience and Indian Rubber.'

Some buildings and streets designed by William H. Playfair:

City Observatory, Calton Hill, 1818; The Calton Scheme, 1819; Royal Terrace, Regent Terrace, Carlton Terrace, Hillside Crescent, Elm Row, Leopold Place, Blenheim Place, Windsor Street, Brunswick Street; University of Edinburgh, Old Quad (outside of quadrangle by Robert Adam, inside by W.H.Playfair) 1819-27; Surgeon's Hall, Nicolson Street, 1829-32; Royal Scottish Academy, 1822-26 and 1831-36; Duddingston Manse, octagonal studio and curling house called 'Edinburgh', 1823; No.8 Inverleith Row, a villa for Dr. Daniel Ellis; National Monument, Calton Hill (with C.R.Cockerell, unfinished), 1824; Challenger Lodge (St Columba's Hospice), St Boswall Road, 1825; Playfair Monument, Calton Hill, 1825; Grange House, restored for Sir Thomas Dick Lauder, 1827; Belmont, Belmont Avenue, Italianate villa for Judge, Lord Joshua Mackenzie, 1828; St Stephen's Church, St Vincent Street,

1827-28; Gatehouse, George Heriot's School, 1829; Dugald Stewart's Greek Doric Temple, Calton Hill, 1831; Craigcrook Castle, major reconstruction for Lord Jeffrey, 1835; Bonaly Towers for Lord Cockburn, 1836; Donaldson's School for the Deaf, West Coates, 1841-51; Lauriston Castle in Cramond Road South, gabled porches on south and west, 1845 and Lodge, 1846; New College and Assembly Hall, Mound Place, 1845-50.

10 *Allan Ramsay Monument*

Passing by William Playfair's Greek Doric design — the Royal Scottish Academy, and across The Mound to West Princes Street Gardens, the first monument is that of Allan Ramsay the Scottish poet whose son, also Allan, was a distinguished painter. The monument, in white Carrara marble, is another by Sir John Steell and was erected in 1848. Behind his monument, looking towards the Castle, is picturesque Ramsay Garden where the poet lived in his 'Goose Pie' House.

Allan Ramsay was born at Leadhills in Lanarkshire in 1686; his father was a mine manager for Lord Hopetoun and his mother was from Derbyshire. Young Allan was apprenticed to a wigmaker and after five years training he opened his own shop in the Grassmarket but his main interest was in writing poetry and satire.

He founded the 'Easy Club' in Edinburgh in 1712 and within a short time he had become well known in literary circles. He wrote two cantos to the humorous Scots poem, *Christ's Kirk on the Green* which was followed by *Tartana*, or *The Plaid*. He was said to have been secretly sympathetic to the Jacobite Cause and hoped for success in the Rising of 1715. From his shop, opposite Niddry Street in the Old Town, he wrote and published *The Gentle Shepherd* and other poems. About this time, 1718, he started his bookselling business from which he lent books — he has the distinction of starting the first lending library in Scotland (1725) and his shop became a popular meeting-place for the literati who enjoyed Ramsay's witty stories and lively conversation. From his shop in the Luckenbooths he wrote and printed his poems each day and many a youngster, clutching a penny, was sent for 'Allan Ramsay's last piece'. He remained in business there until 1752 and became known affectionately as 'honest Allan'.

His collected edition of poems profited him by £420 in 1721 (about £70,000 today) and in the years to 1737 his works included *Fables and Tales*, *Fair Assembly*, a poem *titled Health* and four volumes of songs — *The Tea-table Miscellany* which ran to twelve editions. This was followed shortly afterwards by *The Evergreen*, a collection of Scottish poems written in 1600, and his best work. It included *Hardyknute, a Fragment*, which was discovered in a vault in Dunfermline by Sir John Hope (it was to be read and memorised by young Walter Scott about sixty years later). *The Gentle Shepherd, a Pastoral Comedy* was published in 1725 and dedicated to the astonishingly beautiful Susanna, Countess of Eglinton. In this year he opened his circulating library, but the magistrates, fearing that the spread of fictional literature would somehow corrupt the young, tried unsuccessfully to close it down.

He was now comparatively rich and, again aggravating the authorities, he ignored convention and built a theatre at the foot of Carrubbers Close in 1736. He was in love with the theatre and was passionately keen to encourage drama to a wide audience, but soon after the opening of his theatre an Act of Parliament was passed which required theatres to be licenced. He was refused a licence and forced to close his theatre, much to the satisfaction of the clergy and heavy financial loss to Ramsay.

He designed his own house about 1740, Ramsay Lodge just below the Castle Esplanade. One of his favourite pastimes was to amuse his daughters and their friends for whom he invented many games and made toys. He amused them for hours and each year he gave them a ball, again to the disgruntlement of the clergy. Grant in his Old and New Edinburgh relates the words of one of the young ladies, Mrs Murray of Henderland who, in 1840 approaching her hundredth year, recalled the days of her childhood:

He was charming, he entered so heartily into the plays of the children. He, in particular, gained their hearts by making houses for their dolls. How pleasant it was to learn that our great pastoral poet was a man who, in his privatecapacity, loved to sweeten the daily life of his fellow creatures, and particularly the young.

During his lifetime he saw the birth and growth of the 'Scottish Enlightenment' and the influence of such geniuses as David Hume (1711-76) — the great philosopher and historian, Adam Smith (1723-90) — the father of modern economics; James Hutton (1726-97) — the prominent geologist; architects Robert (1728-92) and James (1730-94) Adam; Adam Ferguson (1723-1816) — the sociologist; Joseph Black (1728-99) — the chemist who developed the theory of 'latent heat'; William Robertson (1721-93) — the modern historiographer; William Cullen (1710-90) — the great teacher of clinical medicine; Henry Home (Lord Kaimes, 1696-1782) — philosopher and judge; James Burnett (Lord Monboddo 1714-99) — anthropologist and judge and Thomas Reid (1710-96) — the head of the Scottish school of philosophy. It was said by Mr Amyat, the King's Chemist, that one could stand in the High Street, 'at the Cross of Edinburgh and, in a few minutes, take fifty men of genius and learning by the hand', an observation made only a few years after Ramsay's death.

Allan Ramsay died in 1758, just at the start of the 'Golden Age' to which he had given impetus. He was buried in Greyfriars Churchyard and his house was inherited by his son, the eminent portrait painter to George III.

11 Scots Greys Boer War Memorial

Immediately opposite Frederick Street is the magnificent monument of a mounted trooper by Birnie Rhind (1906). It commemorates the Royal Scots Greys Regiment of the Boer War (1899-1902).

The fame of the Scots Greys stretches much further back than the Boer War; their origin emanates from a command by Charles II to the Privy Council of Scotland to raise an army capable of dealing with the Covenanters who persistently disobeyed the Act of Parliament which forbade their field conventicles. Three troops were raised in the Borders and commanded by Lieutenant-General Tam Dalziel of the Binns in Linlithgowshire. These were Border's men; they knew each other well and their officers were not the usual aristocrats — this was a family regiment whose first major action was at the Battle of Bothwell Bridge (1679) in which Dalziel refused to serve under Charles II's illegitimate son, the Duke of Monmouth. The Covenanters' leaders held such differing views of religion they prayed against each other and were routed.

This Borders Regiment became the Scots Greys so named because of the grey horses which they were to ride for 300 years. They distinguished themselves in the war against Louis XIV in the War of the Spanish Succession, under Marlborough at a famous victory at Blenheim in 1704 (see also Blenheim Place, Capital Walk 3, number 6 on page 198) then at Ramillies in 1706 where they captured the French Colours of the Regiment du Roi. They added to their battle honours at Oudenarde (1708), Malplaquet (1709), Dettingen (1743), Warburb and Willens (1794). In the latter French resistance was tough; their squares held until an officer of the Scots Greys crashed through making a gap through which his men unhesitatingly rode. Other French squares gave way and victory was assured.

In the Revolutionary and Napoleonic Wars (1793-1815) the Scots Greys fought in many of Admiral Nelson's campaigns. Nelson was killed at Tragalgar in 1805 and at his funeral procession which stretched from Whitehall to St Paul's, the Scots Greys had the distinction of leading the military regiments.

At Waterloo (1815) the Greys earned the soubriquet 'The Bird-Catchers'; with the Union Brigade they charged the French and Sergeant Ewart captured the French Eagle. The trophy was brought home to The Royal Hospital, Chelsea where it remained until 1956. On Waterloo Day, 18th June of that year, the Eagle trophy was transferred with military ceremony to the headquarters of the Scots Greys in Edinburgh Castle.

The Greys won battle honours in the Crimean War of 1854 and suffered heavy loss of life in the freezing trenches and from disease at Balaklava and Sebastopol. In the Boer War the Scots Greys led a full cavalry charge against the Boers; this was the last such attack undertaken by the British army. But they were also the first to adopt the use of camouflage — a lesson learned from the Boers. Under General John French, the unbeaten cavalry commander, they relieved Kimberley and drove off Cronje's forces after fierce fighting to defeat them at Paardeburg in 1900 — this battle is commemorated by this equestrian statue. The Greys went on to gain twenty-six battle honours in the Great War of 1914-18 and a further twenty in World War II of 1939-45.

The Scots Greys united with the 3rd Carabiniers on 2nd July 1971 at Holyrood House — this is the Regimental birthday. The Regimental insignia of the Scots Greys is the badge of the Order of the Thistle with its motto: *Nemo me impune lacessit* — no one provokes me with impunity, and it is now the central design on the Standard of the Royal Scots Dragoon Guards.

A custom specially accorded to the officers of Scots Greys and the 3rd Dragoon Guards concerns the drinking of the Loyal Toast — George III dined regularly with their officers and relaxed in their company; he so enjoyed it that he dispensed with formality of rising to the Loyal Toast. This is therefore the only Regiment in the British Army which remains seated during the Loyal Toast!

12 Dr Thomas Guthrie Monument

Opposite Castle Street stands the monument to the Rev Thomas Guthrie DD by sculptor F.W. Pomeroy in 1910. He is portrayed as a strong, kindly man with his right arm and hand on the shoulder of a small poor boy and in his left hand is the Bible. The portrayal is entirely accurate. Guthrie was the architect, the prime mover, the persuader and the inspi-

ration of the Original Schools. In 1847 he took over rooms in Ramsay Lane off Castle Hill to provide food, clothing and education for seven boys whose poverty was such that they would have received neither sustenance nor education. After only one year he was making similar if not better provision for almost four hundred boys and girls — a phenomenal feat of organisation, persuasion and dedication to the poor.

Guthrie's concept of education was based on a simple but practical philosophy to be quoted often: 'Patience, Prayer and Porridge: porridge first and the other two might follow'. The idea of Ragged Schools soon developed and spread all over Scotland especially when the Education (Scotland) Act of 1872 transferred the administration of education from the church to School Boards in all Parishes and Burghs with powers to levy rates to provide the money for the administration of the existing schools and to provide additional schools with the main aim of eliminating illiteracy.

Thomas Guthrie was born on 12th July 1803 at Brechin in the County of Angus. He studied medicine at the University of Edinburgh and while extending his studies in Paris he was confronted, for the first time, with appalling poverty which caused him to change course towards religion. He became a licenced minister in 1825. His first charge was at Arbirlot near Arbroath and in 1837 he transferred to Old Greyfriars in Edinburgh where, with great energy, he campaigned against Patronage in the Church and became a leader of the 'Disruption' in 1843. The momentous 'walk out' of 470 churchmen from the General Assembly of the Church of Scotland was the final protest against the system of control and choice of the parish minister by the laird or major landowner in each parish. Instead ministers and their congregations wanted democracy in the church; the selection of the minister must be the choice of the congregation and not the whim of a rich patron. The Free Church was formed and Guthrie took charge of the Free Church of St John's, now St Columba's Church in Johnston Terrace.

In 1847 Guthrie published his frighteningly enlightening, Plea for Ragged Schools; this was received with great public approbation. He was convinced that many of the extremes of poverty were exacerbated by the over-plentiful supplies of alcoholic drink available at almost any hour in any place. He became a total abstainer and gave his strong support to the Forbes-Mackenzie Act which curtailed the opening hours of public houses and closed them on Sundays. He felt the gratitude of many distraught mothers whose children had starved because of their hard drinking fathers. The social conditions of Edinburgh were graphically described in his book, *The City: its Sins and Sorrows* published in 1857.

Guthrie raised the huge sum of £116,000 for the Manse Scheme for homeless ministers; many landowners had evicted their Parish Ministers if they professed support for the Free Church. In 1872 he was elected Moderator of the Free Church of Scotland. When Dr Thomas Guthrie died at his home in Salisbury Road on 24th February 1873, aged seventy, it was cause for national mourning. It seemed that the whole of Edinburgh attended his funeral; he was buried in the Grange Cemetery and was survived by his ten children (his sixth son became the well-known judge, Lord Guthrie). Fifteen years after he died a school for boys was opened at Lasswade Road and sixteen years after that another school bearing his name was opened for girls at Gilmerton; it is now a Community Centre.

13 Sir James Simpson Statue

The last statue in West Princes Street Gardens is that of Sir James Young Simpson after whom the Simpson Maternity Pavilion is named. He was the caring gynaecologist and obstetrician who helped to take the pain out of surgery. In 1847 he discovered the anaesthetic power of chloroform.  His statue, by William Brodie in 1876, is immediately west of that of Dr Thomas Guthrie. It is the tribute of this city to a surgeon so dedicated that he literally worked himself to death at the age of fifty-nine.

James Young Simpson was born in 1811 at Bathgate, the youngest son of a baker. He studied medicine at the University of Edinburgh and as a student he witnessed the horror, the unbelievable agony and the subsequent debility, sometimes permanent, that many patients suffered at the hands of the surgeon's knife. He could not accept that the profession he was about to enter could perpetuate such suffering.

He knew, of course, of Sir Humphrey Davy's discovery of nitrous oxide (laughing gas) and that Horace Wells, an American dentist, had a tooth extracted from his own mouth without pain under this gas. This was 1844 and Simpson had already established his reputation in hospital reform; he virtually founded gynaecology and he had been appointed to the Chair of Midwifery at the age of twenty-nine. He was desperately keen to alleviate the pains of childbirth. Two more years were to pass before an American surgeon reluctantly allowed a young dentist, Dr Wilton Morton (Wells' partner) to administer sulphurous ether for an operation with complete success and without pain from the surgeon's scalpel. But ether had side effects — irritation of the lungs and post operative nausea for several days; as a result only a few surgeons would use it.

Simpson was busily experimenting with several options and a new, volatile compound — chloroform. It was at his home at No.52 Queen Street, after a dinner party with some medical colleagues, that they decided to experiment with a few drugs. Most of them were ineffective and almost as a last resort Simpson suggested chloroform; he poured a few drops on a cloth and applied it over the mouth and nose of each of his doctor friends. There was no thought of danger. Initially the doctors present, Duncan, Keith and Simpson himself, became unusually talkative and animated, then suddenly they passed out and slept for a while. Simpson woke first and was able to observe his colleagues — there were no after effects; it was a remarkable success. From that day in November 1847 Simpson used chloroform for his patients in the maternity wards, the example being set by the Queen and the Ladies of the Court. In 1853 it was used at the birth of Prince Leopold which gave it the Royal seal of approval. However, the use of chloroform was a new innovation and the medical establishment was unsure and the Church showed signs of disapproval. It took some years before it was used for all operations; then it was hailed as the marvel of the age — at last, painless surgery due to the persistent persuasion of this dedicated doctor.

He was made a Baronet by Queen Victoria but it made little difference to his busy life of teaching, inventing, writing, debating, entertaining and travelling. His house in Queen Street was said to be 'more like a busy station than a restful abode.' They packed the place — doctors, patients, distinguished foreigners and cranks — he could not get peace even to eat; but he enjoyed every minute of it. He took no exercise, his dietary and sleeping habits were so spasmodic that he neglected himself abominably and paid the price of an early death at age fifty-nine on 5th May 1870.

14 Hope Street

At the west end of Princes Street, the last street which leads to Charlotte Square is Hope Street, the west side of which has been left largely unadulterated. The main doors are beautifully arched with fanlights and the double bow and matching dormers are preserved. Hope Street is named after Charles Hope of Granton, Lord Granton (1763-1851), who was appointed Lord Advocate in 1801, Lord Justice Clerk in 1804, Lord President of the Court of Session in 1811 and was Tory MP for the City of Edinburgh.

Charles Hope was born on 29th June 1763, his father was John Hope, MP for Linlithgowshire, a grandson of the 1st Earl of Hopetoun. Young Charles was educated at Enfield Grammar School and at the High School in Edinburgh; a very bright pupil, he was Latin dux in 1777. He studied law at the University of Edinburgh and was admitted to the Faculty of Advocates in 1784 and, although he was not particularly well known as a lawyer, he was a powerful orator for the Tories. He was appointed Depute Advocate in 1786 and in 1792 he was made Sheriff of Orkney.

In 1793, amid the clamour of war against the French, he married his cousin, Lady Charlotte, second daughter of John, 2nd Earl of Hopetoun; they had four sons and eight daughters. When the Volunteer movement was formed Hope, full of enthusiasm, joined as a private in what was called the 'Gentlemen Volunteers' — the 1st Regiment of the Edinburgh Volunteers. He rose to the rank of Lieutenant-Colonel and was described by Lord Cockburn, in his *Memorials* as 'almost the only ardent spirit among them.'

In 1801 Prime Minister William Pitt resigned, George III's insanity coincided with the change of government and the new Addington administration appointed Hope as Lord Advocate. His success in obtaining the Poor's Bill for Edinburgh was rewarded by giving him the Freedom of the City. In 1802 Addington called a General Election and Hope was elected MP for Dumfries; however he resigned this seat when Henry Dundas was elevated to the House of Lords and Hope was elected unopposed as MP for the City of Edinburgh. He steered the Scotch Parochial Schoolmasters Act through the Commons. This Act required all parish landowners, much to their annoyance, to provide a two-room house for schoolmasters.

After Charles Hope's appointment as a Lord of Session in 1804 he replaced Sir David Rae, Lord Eskgrove, as Lord Justice Clerk and assumed the title, Lord Granton. His appointment, in 1811, as Lord President of the Court of Session, succeeding Lord Blair of Avontoun, was something of a surprise in judicial circles as it was widely anticipated that the more senior and popular Henry Erskine would be appointed. But Charles Hope was a man of considerable charisma, an imposing presence and with a deep melodious voice he compelled attention. In his *Memorials* Cockburn recalled:

> It is a pleasure for me to think of Hope. He was my first, I might say my only, professional patron, and used to take me with him on his circuits; and in spite of my obstinate and active Whiggery, he has been kind to me through life. When his son, who was Solicitor-General in 1830, lost his office by the elevation of the Reformed Ministry, and I succeeded him, his father shook me warmly by the hand, and said, 'Well Harry, I wish you joy. Since my son was to lose it, I am glad that your father's son has got it.'

When James Graham, 3rd Duke of Montrose, died in 1836 his office of Lord Justice was amalgamated with that of the Lord President and Charles Hope had that office devolved upon him by an enactment of George IV and William IV. Charles Hope retired from the Bench in 1841; he died ten years later and was buried in the family mausoleum at Hopetoun House.

15 Charlotte Square

From Hope Street we enter the magnificence of Charlotte Square. Its designer, the most famous architect of his day, was Robert Adam in 1791. The first feu was taken in March the following year and Adam died a few days afterwards. Charlotte Square was the completion of James Craig's plan in which it was named St George's Square but changed so that it would not be confused with George Square in the South Side. The name Charlotte Square was approved in 1786 commemorating the wife of George III.

Before giving a brief biography of Queen Charlotte it is worth enumerating some of the houses and some of their eminent occupants. For example, on the west side at No.16 Alexander Graham Bell, the inventor of the telephone, was born in 1857 and at No.14 lived Lord Cockburn, the famous Whig jurist who became Solicitor General and wrote his often quoted Memorials. West Register House, originally St George's Church, was designed by Robert Reid in 1811 to a simplified version of Robert Adam's original in an attempt to economise.

On the north side David Watson Stevenson the sculptor lived at No.1 the interior of which he designed himself and is one of the finest in the City. No.5 was the birthplace of Leander Starr Jameson, the close friend of Cecil Rhodes who led the abortive 'Jameson Raid' on the Boers in South Africa but was captured and imprisoned. The house was purchased by the Marquis of Bute and restored in Adam style; Nos. 5,6 and 7 were released in part payment of death duties in 1956 after the death of the 5th Marquis. No.5 is the headquarters of the National Trust for Scotland. No.6, Bute House, is the official residence of the Secretary of State for Scotland. No.7 is also owned by the Trust; it is well-known as 'The Georgian House' and well worth visiting to understand bourgeois life in late 18th century Edinburgh. Its upper floors were restored by the Baird Trust for the official residence of the Moderator of the General Assembly of the Church of Scotland. No.9 was the home of Lord Joseph Lister (1827-1912) who gave new life to the procedures of surgery with his introduction of antiseptics in 1860.

Continuing round to the north-east side, No.45

CHARLOTTE SQUARE, DESIGNED BY ROBERT ADAM

was occupied by another eminent doctor, Sir Robert Philip who is credited with the elimination of the dreaded disease tuberculosis. No.44 was the home and business premises of architect Robert Reid who designed it for himself with a perfect view of St George's Church which he designed in 1811 (using much of Adam's 1791 design). On the south side Field Marshal Earl Haig, Commander-in-Chief of the British Army during World War I, was born at No.25; his equestrian statue is on the north side of the Castle Esplanade.

The square and streets, including Queen Charlotte Street in Leith, were named after Queen Charlotte Sophia, the wife of George III. Born in the year 1744, she was the youngest daughter of Charles Lewis, brother of the Duke of Mecklenberg-Strelitz (a small German state). Although George was in love with Lady Sarah Lennox, Princess Charlotte was considered a more suitable choice to become Queen of Great Britain. As a young lady she wrote to the King of Prussia pleading with him to prevent his army from their devastation of the countryside. This letter brought her name to the attention of the English Court as a suitable consort for George III. She landed in England on 7th September 1761 after ten days at sea and met George for the first time. They were married that night and their coronation took place two weeks later.

Horace Walpole, 4th Earl of Orford, described her:

'She is not tall or a beauty. Pale and very thin; but looks sensible and genteel … she talks a great deal and French tolerably'. Her marriage was happy at first and she gave birth to fifteen children; the eldest, Charlotte Augusta Matilda, married the future King of Wurtemberg. Some of her nine sons were a disappointment and she had cause to express her disapproval, exasperation and anger because of their excesses in spending, gambling and womanising. She had no influence over politics which she probably did not understand. She had few of the social niceties and was devoid of humour; life at Court was extremely dull. Her early training made her mean with money which was agreeable to the King who lived almost frugally. For instance, she insisted on using every apple from the royal orchard to make her Apple-Charlotte. But she was happy; she was heard to declare: 'Since my marriage I have never known a moment of real sorrow.' However, her later life with George III became more difficult as he was increasingly at odds with his sons and with his Prime Ministers and although he was clean-living, religious and extremely patriotic, he was stubborn.

In 1788 the King's mental health deteriorated and Queen Charlotte's real strength became very evident; she took over the complete running of the household and the total care of her husband. She brooked no interference. In 1810 their favourite daughter, Amelia, died: this seemed to exacerbate George's insanity which now became permanent. The worst fears of the Government were now realised: the Prince of Wales had to be made Regent in 1812, he was forty-eight years old and for the next two years life at Court was hectic. Queen Charlotte's pleas of moderation were ignored.

The next eighteen years of her life were quite tragic: the scorn of her sons and the goading of George's political opponents only served to increase the stress of her existence. She continued to care for her husband without help and as a result of overwork and anxiety she died at Kew on 17th November 1818 aged seventy-four, two years before her husband who never realised her passing. She was buried in St George's Chapel, Windsor.

16 Prince Albert Monument

The Albert Memorial, in the middle of the octagon-shaped garden of Charlotte Square, is a 30ft/9m high equestrian figure of the Prince Consort in the uniform of a Field Marshal. Its huge granite plinth has quotations and episodes of his life in bas-relief and at each corner are groups of mourners. It was designed by John Steell who was knighted by Queen Victoria at its unveiling in 1876, fifteen years after Albert's death.

Albert, a peace-loving man, worked himself to the point of exhaustion in politics but he was regarded as interfering and was mistrusted by Lord Palmerston and the Whigs. He encouraged the arts, social improvements and industrial innovation. The Great Exhibition of 1851 was his all-consuming interest. He brought the Christmas tree to Britain complete with candles and artificial snow. But more important was his deep concern for the plight of the working man.

Albert, born on 28th August 1819, was three months younger than Victoria. His father, Ernest, was Duke of Saxe-Coburg-Gotha whose treatment of his children verged on cruelty. His mother, Louisa, was the daughter of the Duke of Saxe-Coburg-Altenburg, who ran off with a lieutenant when Albert was five years of age. Albert, their second son, was educated at Brussels and Bonn — a serious-minded, very studious and laboriously intellectual student; he was strongly attracted towards an academic career. He brought a German style monarchy to Britain which was not particularly popular. He was not allowed admission to the Queen's interviews with her ministers in spite of his claim to be her 'permanent minister'. This mistrust was partly due to his adherence to the influence of his mentor, Baron Stockmar, who expounded at length his Germanic ideas of monarchical government; for example, he considered that Queen Victoria should have the power of veto on any nomination of Prime Minister. In fact, Victoria and Albert tried to get rid of Palmerston but did not succeed.

Two years after their marriage in 1840 the Queen made Albert, Consort. They had nine children of whom he was inordinately proud and took a fanatical interest in their health, welfare and education. Their marriages were arranged to suit the dynasty rather than any preference they expressed. Albert was not particularly religious and regarded the inactivity and boredom of Victorian Sundays with disgust and, against Church and public opinion, he preferred to take his family on playful but educational adventures. He was never at ease with English aristocracy; he preferred the company of 'experts' — technologists, scientists and artists. The royal finances, which had always been in a chaotic state, were brought into efficient order by Albert.

He set out to 'discover' Britain and almost dragged Victoria along; he was appalled at the living conditions of the workers — he gave Victoria a social conscience especially when he became President of the Society of the Labouring classes in which capacity he clashed fiercely with Prime Minister Lord John Russell and he actively supported Lord Shaftesbury to improve the conditions of the poor. At that time (1856) the River Thames was in a filthy state — it carried London's sewerage. London itself had no sewers; disease — cholera, typhus, etc, was prevalent — the Thames water was disparagingly referred to as 'aqua mortis'. Albert pestered politicians year after year until eventually it was agreed to build proper sewers.

Albert was undoubtedly the champion of the working man; he could not understand the huge gap in living standards between the rich industrialists and the workers who created their wealth. His speeches put him on the side of the Radicals but he was a Peelite who believed, passionately, in the preservation of society and he succeeded in bringing about many improvements in the provinces.

Cambridge University surprised him for its almost medieval curriculum — no sciences or humanities were taught — he revolutionised that university. He was a thoroughly modern man, a devotee of science and technology, manufacture and the arts and he successfully fused them together in the Great Exhibition of 1851 in Hyde Park. So much so, that his sponsorship and active management ensured its success in the display of Britain as the world leader in manufactured goods. The exhibition was housed in Joseph Paxton's masterpiece of architecture — the Crystal Palace, which tragically burned down in 1936. Its 33 million cubic feet of structure was built by two thousand workers in eighteen days. It was opened by Queen Victoria on 1st May 1851 as a peace festival bringing unity to all nations. The upper classes paid two guineas entry but Albert's idea of the one shilling ticket on Mondays and Thursdays brought in four million visitors and a profit of £186,000 which paid for London's Albert Hall.

Albert loved Scotland — the acquisition of of Balmoral in 1852 was largely his initiative as was Osborne House in the Isle of Wight where many happy family holidays were spent. In 1857 he was made Prince Consort but in his last years he fell into a deep depression and felt a failure in his political aims; his obsession against Palmerston and against the Crimean War brought public opinion against him — crowds gathered at the Tower of London when it was rumoured that he had been imprisoned. Albert had worked himself to death; tragically he was struck down by one of the diseases he had worked so hard to

PRINCE ALBERT MONUMENT WITH DETAIL (BELOW) FROM THE BASE

eradicate — typhus fever. He died aged only forty-two at Windsor Castle on 14th December 1861. Victoria mourned deeply; she became a tragic, lonely figure for many years.

17 George Street

Leaving Charlotte Square and walking east along George Street we find ourselves in the city's most prestigious street, wide enough to take the turning-circle of a carriage and four horses — this is what was intended in James Craig's original plan. It was, with Royal consent, named after King George III. Great King Street, the central avenue of Northern New Town, is also named after George III.

George III's long reign (1760-1820) spanned several decades of great change: politically, industrially and socially — the French Revolution (1789), the ultimate defeat of Napoleon (1815), the loss of the American colonies (1776), the invention of the improved steam engine (1774), the new empire of India (1773), the publication of Adam Smith's Wealth of Nations (1776) and the changes in economic policy and the industrial revolution in which Britain became the workshop of the world. Ironically George III was an inflexible and stubborn man who saw no need for change — he imagined that all around him was quite perfect.

George III was born in 1738, eldest son of Frederick Louis, Prince of Wales who predeceased his father, George II, and so George III succeeded his grandfather in the year 1760. He was the first Hanoverian king to be to be born and educated in England and the first to gain the respect of the people. He reigned for fifty years and during the last ten years of his life he was blind and insane and his eldest, dissolute, disrespectful son was appointed Regent until he was crowned in 1820.

Before becoming king, George was thought to have been deeply in love with a Quaker girl, Hannah Lightfoot, by whom he was said to have had a daughter. He wanted to marry Lady Sarah Lennox but Parliament and protocol required that he marry Princess Charlotte of Mecklenberg-Strelitz (a little known German state). They had fifteen children; nine sons and six daughters. George III and his eldest son quarrelled continuously, partly because the king was over-protective and partly over the prince's excesses.

The King set an example of simple tastes; he liked the outdoor life and simple food; he wrote several pamphlets on the subject of agricultural improvements. He was at least the intellectual equal of other monarchs in Europe. He wanted not simply to reign but to govern his country; he was passionately patriotic but his 'personal government' between 1763 and 1782 was disastrous while he imagined it to be flawless. He vehemently disagreed with Prime Minister William Pitt the elder, partly because of his collaboration with the Prince of Wales in opposing him. However, Lord North's twelve years of office (1770 to 1782) pleased him, mainly because he could get his own way, North having been a boyhood friend and who had been well taught to ensure that the king was not displeased.

On 4th July 1776, the American colonies, having declared North's taxation on imported goods intolerable, declared their independence, but it was George III's stubborn adherence to a policy of no concessions to the Americans that prolonged their struggle. After Cornwallis capitulated at Yorktown on 19th October 1781, rather than accept their independence, George III threatened abdication.

When Pitt the Younger became Prime Minister in 1784, at age twenty-five, the King was triumphant — the power of the old Whig families was at last ended. Pitt's election victory was decisive and for almost twenty years he led the nation through difficult times. The King's view of the French Revolution (1789) was of equanimity — he considered that the House of Bourboun deserved it for their excesses and for their support of the rebels of the Thirteen Colonies — the Revolution therefore, he considered Divine intervention. However, there were assassination attempts against him; on 15th May 1800 two pistol shots were fired at him in the royal box at Drury Lane Theatre. They narrowly missed and he calmly signalled that the performance should continue; he fell asleep during the interval.

It was about 1788 that George III's 'illness' first began; during a dinner at Windsor he attacked his eldest son and afterwards talked gibberish and foamed at the mouth. His treatment was tantamount to cruelty but his doctors thought it for his benefit; he was bound in a straight jacket and either tied to his bed or to a special iron chair. Painful blisters were induced on his skin by means of poultices of Spanish Fly and mustard in the belief that the 'evil humours' would be drawn from his body. The thought that he might die brought panic to the stock exchange; the Prince of Wales's succession was unimaginable. George III recovered and his subsequent tour of the South of England in 1789 was a great success.

Prime Minister Pitt resigned when the King refused to allow Catholic emancipation as a concomitant of the Union with Ireland in 1801, but he took up office again and was hailed the saviour of the nation after the victory over the French at Trafalgar (1805) when Nelson gave his life. Pitt died of overwork a year later. By this time the King was suffering from more frequent bouts of insanity; he was said to have shaken hands with the branch of an oak tree imagining it to be a foreign ambassador. His favourite daughter, Princess Amelia, died in 1810 and his grief exacerbated his mental state to such an extent that Parliament reluctantly appointed the dissolute Prince of Wales as Regent.

In 1820 George III died tragically aged eighty-two — lonely, blind and insane but even though his political opponents ridiculed him he was well loved by his people as a good king.

18 Thomas Chalmers Statue

At the junction of George Street and Frederick Street stands the statue of the Rev Thomas Chalmers DD, described as one of the most remarkable men of the century — 'never did Scotland produce a greater or more lovable soul'. It is a bronze on a red granite plinth by Sir John Steell in 1878.

Thomas Chalmers led the 'Disruption' in 1843 when his stirring speech at the General Assembly of the Church of Scotland was enough to convince 470 churchmen that the time had come to rebel against patronage in the Church. They were applauded when they appeared, en masse, from the portals of St Andrews Church in George Street. Chalmers was insistent that ministers of the Church should be chosen by their congregations rather than through the patronage of the rich and powerful who as landowners of their parishes had complete authority to hire and fire their Parish Ministers.

Chalmers was an amazing man; not only was he an inspiring preacher but he was an equally gifted teacher of chemistry and mathematics and, in 1803, when he was Assistant Professor of Mathematics at the University of St Andrews his extra-mural lectures were very popular and in great demand. At that time he was minister of Kilmany Church in north Fife not far from St Andrews. He was born at Anstruther in 1780, where his father was a successful merchant and shipowner, and educated in the Universities of St Andrews and Edinburgh.

In his *Memorials of His Time*, Lord Cockburn described Chalmers thus:

In point of mere feature, it would not be difficult to think him ugly. But he is saved from this, and made interesting and lovable, by singular modesty, kindness and simplicity of manner, a strong expression of calm thought and benevolence ... In spite of a bad figure, voice, gesture and look, and an unusual plainness of Scotch accent, Chalmers is a great orator, at the moment of speaking, unapproached in our day ... Nothing that I could say would express one half of my affectionate and reverential admiration of this great man.

He became Parish Minister in a poor area of Glasgow, the Tron, and, while he was Convenor of the Church Expansion Committee, he raised almost one-third of a million pounds — a phenomenal sum for those days (about £30 million today) — to build 220 new churches. Some of his magnificent sermons were published as Astronomical Discourses and his Commercial Discourses in 1820 was an immediate success. After eight years in Glasgow he was appointed to the Chair of Moral Philosophy in St Andrews and then to the Chair of Theology in Edinburgh University. The University of Oxford honoured him with a Doctorate of Civil Law in 1834.

The district of Church Hill, according to William Mair, was given its name when Dr. Chalmers built his house at No.2 Morningside Place; he was then Professor of Divinity at the University. He strongly promoted the need for a Parish Church in Morningside; the nearest being St Cuthbert's in Lothian Road. He moved to another house at No.1 Church Hill and, soon afterwards, the arguments between Church and State reached breakdown with the 'Disruption'. Under his guidance and with untiring energy the Free Church became quickly successful in a spirit of new hope and reform after its separation from the Church of Scotland in 1843. He founded the New College of the Free Church and was appointed its first Principal and Professor of Divinity.

He died suddenly at his home in Church Hill, aged sixty-seven on 31st May 1847, the day after he returned from the House of Commons where he had been pleading the case against the refusal of Scottish landowners to sell land for some of his new churches. He was buried in Grange Cemetery.

19 William Pitt Statue

Continuing along George Street, at the intersection with Frederick Street the statue of William Pitt, 2nd Earl of Chatham, the youngest ever British Prime Minister, was erected in 1833 and was sculpted by Sir Francis Chantrey.

Pitt became a Member of Parliament aged twenty-two and a year later, 1782, he was appointed Chancellor of the Exchequer. He declined a tempting offer from George III of the premiership with total freedom to choose his cabinet. He became Prime Minister in 1784 to form a ministry which lasted almost twenty years and during which he is credited with the construction of the modern British State.

William Pitt was born in 1759 at Hayes near Bromley. He was the second son of the Earl of Chatham. Educated by tutors, his first taste of formal education, aged fourteen, was at Pembroke Hall, Cambridge, where he proved his excellence as a classical scholar.

He was called to the Bar in June 1780 and was given the Parliamentary seat of Appleby by Sir James Lowther. Immediately, he condemned the 'diabolical' American War and he quickly gained an enormous reputation as an outstanding orator, but his bill for Parliamentary Reform and his proposals for the elimination of abuses in public offices were unsuccessful. The King dismissed the Cabinet having vetoed their stupid proposal to give £100,000 (about £12 million today) to his spendthrift son, the Prince of Wales. Pitt again became Chancellor of the Exchequer and First Lord of the Treasury; his emergency Cabinet had over one hundred votes against it but his unrivalled Parliamentary skill and determination won over most of the Independents so that, in March 1784 when he dissolved

Parliament, the ensuing election gave him a powerful majority.

His principal opponent, Charles James Fox, lost seventy of his followers. This government lasted seventeen years. Pitt was twenty-five years old and Fox, ten years his senior, was his adversary throughout. Their policies were broadly similar — parliamentary reform, appeasement with Irish Catholics and hatred of slavery; but Fox was a drinking, gambling womaniser, whereas Pitt was an idealist who believed in the virtue of hard work. Both were brilliantly eloquent in debate — never before, or perhaps since, had Parliament witnessed such scintillatingly inspired speeches.

Pitt was now the most powerful minister in the history of Parliament and as premier he steadily got rid of the worst corruption and many Whig sinecures; these changes gave Parliament greater constitutional significance and more control to the people. The aristocracy were furious when he made ninety-five new peers plus seventy-seven for Ireland. His government inherited a £238 million debt, the interest payments of which took up almost eighty per cent of the revenue. American independence ruined trade and duty on imported goods was ridiculously complex which made smuggling attractive, but in 1786 a beneficial treaty with France was negotiated. In 1789 he tackled the economic problems in consultation with the Kirkcaldy-born Glasgow University Professor of Logic, Adam Smith, who was famous for his publication *An Inquiry into the Nature and Causes of the Wealth of Nations.*

Pitt's attitude to the French Revolution (1789) was neutral and, reluctantly he took up arms when France declared war on 1st February 1793. He wrongly assumed a short war would ensue but the nation's financial reserves were to be depleted to pay for a war which lasted twenty-two years. The situation was further exacerbated with the civil revolution in Ireland and dire poverty in Scotland. There were mass meetings in London, in Sheffield pikes were made; the government suspended habeas corpus in 1794 and bad harvests drove up prices — the cry was 'bread and no war'; even the King was stoned.

In spite of the troubles at home and abroad, Pitt's popularity continued with the election of 1796 but the 'United Englishmen' conspired with the French and

Irish; an invasion was suspected, habeas corpus was again suspended and Pitt fought a duel with the Whig Tierney, accusing him of obstructing public service. Fox was removed from the privy council for toasting the 'sovereignty of the people'.

The war in Europe was going badly in 1800 but Wellesley (later Duke of Wellington) had expanded the British empire in India where his brother, Richard, was Governor-General. Malta too was taken and Sir Ralph Abercrombie successfully landed at Aboukir (where he was unfortunately killed) forcing the French surrender of Egypt while Nelson defeated the Danes at Copenhagen. But it was the Irish problem which proved the downfall of the government. Pitt had tried conciliation with the Catholics; the rebellion, kept down with 45,000 troops, led to a legislative Union and Catholic emancipation. The King was furious and Pitt resigned. George III appointed the Speaker of the House, Henry Addington, as Prime Minister and during his weak Ministry the Peace of Amiens was signed (1802). This lost the United Kingdom the island of Malta, the Cape, the West Indian Islands and Menorca. Britain had no allies, a debt of £290 million and the loss of 3,000 merchant ships. War broke out again and it became obvious that Napoleon was preparing to invade Britain having already taken Hanover.

Pitt had to assure the King that Catholic emancipation would not take place and in 1804 Pitt again formed a Ministry. Meanwhile, Napoleon became Emperor of France; he annexed Genoa and made himself King of Italy. Britain prepared for invasion; Pitt volunteered as Warden of the Cinque Ports, one of 350,000 volunteers. General Mack's forces were defeated by the French at Ulm the day before Nelson gave his life in exchange for a magnificent victory at Trafalgar to save Britain from invasion. Pitt was hailed the saviour of Europe but by the end of the year Napoleon had defeated the Austro-Russian army at Austerlitz, the Czar had retreated from Germany and Britain withdrew from the Baltic. Amid all this calamity, Pitt died from sheer exhaustion in January 1806 aged only forty-six.

20 Frederick Street

The first feus in Frederick Street were granted in 1786, twenty years after James Craig won his gold medal for his design of the New Town. It is part of his grid system of streets and links Princes Street through George Street to Queen Street.

Frederick Street is named after George III's father, Frederick Louis, Prince of Wales, born at Hanover in 1707, the year of the Union of the Scottish and English Parliaments — the age of Hanoverian Kings, of splendid opulence for the rich and squalid poverty for the poor. Frederick was a sickly, pale-faced child and his parents could not stand the sight of him; if anything, his mother Queen Caroline, hated him even more than the King, George II. He was brought up with rigid, authoritarian strictness in the German tradition and he was educated in Germany. He quarrelled incessantly with his father, who kept him isolated in Hanover and short of money — he came to be called 'Poor Fred'. The King compounded their querulousness by choosing a wife for him in spite of the well known fact that Frederick was very fond of Princess Wilhelmina of Prussia who had been the happy preference of his grandfather. The wedding arrangements were in hand but George I died suddenly from a cerebral haemorrhage and as soon as Frederick's father became King, in 1727, he promptly cancelled the marriage negotiations with the vicious remark, 'I did not think that ingrafting my half-witted coxcomb upon a mad woman would improve the breed'. Frederick gave in and married his father's choice, Augusta of Saxe-Gotha.

Relationships between father and son worsened to a point when Frederick impulsively moved out of the paternal home to lodgings in St James's Square at a dangerous time for his wife who was just about to give birth to their son, George William Frederick, who became George III. The King was furious at his son's decision not to allow the forthcoming royal child to be born under his roof. But more embarrassment was to come — there were scandalous rumours that Prime Minister, Sir Robert Walpole, was having an affair with the Queen and Frederick made matters even worse by joining with the opposition group in Parliament against the King thereby hoping to receive a more generous allowance from the Tories than the £24,000 per annum allowed by his father. When Queen Caroline died, a long painful death, George II was heartbroken and Walpole's predominance was weakened.

George II, in open disgust of his eldest son, said of him: 'Our first born is the greatest ass, the greatest liar, the greatest canaille and the greatest beast in the whole world and we heartily wish he was out of it'. Little did he realize that his wish would come true. However, Frederick retaliated: 'He is an obstinate, self-indulgent, miserly martinet with an insatiable sexual appetite'. One thing on which they did agree, for entirely different reasons, was war and in 1739 it started against Spain and then France. George II gleefully led his army in the field, his encouragement to his troops and his victory gained him popularity — previously at a dangerously low ebb. 'Poor Fred's' friends deserted him for the King.

Frederick, although weak and indecisive, even ridiculous at times, was nevertheless artistic and a discerning collector of works of art. He could not be described as vicious or vindictive although he often talked of what he would do when he became king. It was not to be, he died nine years before his father in 1751, only forty-four years of age.

21 *George IV Statue*

At the junction of George Street and Hanover Street the statue of George IV is a bronze by Sir Francis Chantrey in 1831. There are more streets in Edinburgh named in honour of George IV than any other monarch — George IV Bridge, Prince Regent Street, Regent Bridge, Gardens, Lane, Place, Road, Street, Street Lane, Terrace and Terrace Lane, Rothesay Place and Terrace (from his title Duke of Rothesay), Royal Crescent and Terrace (a compliment to his Royal visit to Edinburgh in 1822), Carlton Terrace, Terrace Lane and Mews (from his London residence Carlton House), Chester Street (from his title Earl of Chester), Cornwall Street (from his title Duke of Cornwall), King's Bridge Road and Place, Windsor Terrace, Place and Street (commemorating the 1822 visit). There was no doubt that he captured the imagination of the Edinburgh establishment and the populace during his visit in sumptuous grandeur in 1822 when he paraded through the streets dressed in a Stuart tartan kilt and pink stockings; some jeered but most of the onlookers cheered.

George IV was born in the year 1762, the eldest of nine sons and six daughters. He had a strict upbringing and, whereas his father had simple tastes, he rebelled with extravagances through his gambling, his love affairs and drunkenness. In 1785 he compounded his offensive behaviour by marrying, in secret, a Roman Catholic lady, Mrs Fitzherbert, with whom he was genuinely in love. She had refused to consent to intimacy unless he married her. The marriage was invalid under the 1772 Royal Marriages Act but he denied it in any case. Again, to spite his father, he chose the political association of the Whigs and of those statesmen his father detested — Fox, Burke and Sheridan. Even the Prime Minister, Pitt the elder, sided with the Prince of Wales against George III whose insanity reached maniacal proportions in November 1788; he attacked the Prince of Wales and tried to smash his head against a wall. Pitt's cabinet proposed a Regency Bill; the Prince was almost desperate to reign — he commonly boasted of what he would do when he became Regent and repeatedly slandered his father with stories of his private life long before he had shown signs of insanity. However the Prince's ambitions were frustrated when his father recovered in February 1789 and he had to wait another twelve years before becoming Regent.

His extravagent lifestyle accrued huge debts which totalled £650,000 (almost £100 million today) which Parliament agreed to settle on condition that he settled down and married Princess Caroline, daughter of the Duke of Brunswick. She was no beauty; in fact he was so shocked by her appearance that he drank himself into a stupor for the marriage ceremony in 1795. The match was a disaster; they loathed one another. On their wedding night he was disgustingly drunk and fell asleep with his head in the fireplace. She left him soon after the birth of their only daughter, Charlotte, in 1796 and returned in 1820, when he became King to claim her title.

He had developed an unreasonable hatred for the House of Coburg and, at his insistence, his wife was never recognised as Queen and was refused entry to Westminster Hall at her husband's coronation. He tried to divorce her by accusing her of that of which he was most guilty — adultery. He forced the introduction of a Bill in Parliament which would not only deprive her of the title Queen but would declare her marriage to the King 'forever wholly dissolved, annulled and made void'. Suspect evidence was produced to show her infidelity but the ensuing uproar caused the Bill to be dropped. A London mob threatened to riot in support of her, shouting 'No Queen! No King!', and George cleared out for safety's sake; at one point his life was threatened with assassination. However, she died suddenly on 7th August 1821.

He was furiously angry when Parliament decided that his daughter, Princess Charlotte, should marry King Leopold of the Belgians. Their popularity in England aggravated him and when she died giving birth to a stillborn son there was national sorrow. The succession was now in doubt; George IV had resolutely refused to live with his wife and of his five brothers, two were married but had no family and the others had their allowances threatened by Parliament unless they gave up their mistresses and married to produce a legitimate heir to the throne.

The year after his accession he visited Ireland and Hanover and in 1822 his visit to Scotland was organised by Sir Walter Scott. He was the first crowned head to visit the capital since Charles II in 1650. He spent two weeks inspecting public institutions and receiving the congratulations and adulation of the people who had travelled far in the hope of a glimpse of him. He arrived in Leith on the 15th August and the route of the Royal procession was Leith Walk, Waterloo Place, Regent Road to the Palace of Holyroodhouse. He then proceeded to the Duke of Buccleuch's house at Dalkeith where he resided for his two week visit.

His Regency and reign totalled eighteen years. He could not be trusted politically and was described in *The Times* as 'a hard-drinking, swearing man who at all times would prefer a girl and a bottle to politics and a sermon'. However, when relatively sober his wit and charm were irresistible; he could be positively brilliant and his conversation sparkled.

Towards the end of his life he lived in an almost fantasy world; he even pretended to have played a major part in winning the Battle of Waterloo but whether this was to annoy the ageing Duke of Wellington or whether he believed it himself, no-one quite knew. He lived almost as a recluse at Windsor. He died a tragic figure, aged sixty-eight on 26th June 1830.

22 Hanover Street

Hanover Street, at rightangles to George Street, links Princes Street through to Queen Street. It was completed by 1790 the first feu being taken six years before and was named to commemorate the Royal House of Hanover which came to the throne of Britain in 1714 with George I and continued until the reign of Queen Victoria in 1837.

There were six Hanoverian sovereigns: George I, 1714-27; George II, 1727-60; George III, 1760-1820; George IV, 1820-30; William IV, 1830-37 and Victoria, 1837-1901. She was excluded from the Hanoverian throne because of her sex — only males could accede to the crown of Hanover.

The first Hanoverian King was George I. He was a gruff warrior who could hardly speak English and visited England only rarely; he knew that his choice as king was under sufferance but he was a Protestant and James Edward Stuart, the Old Pretender and son of the feared, hated and deposed James II (VII of Scotland), was a Roman Catholic. George I had been accustomed to the complete unquestioning obedience of his people in Hanover whereas in England he was bound by a constitution and a fractious parliament; he was laughed at because of his Turkish servants, his wish to plant turnips in St James's Park and his preference for ugly mistresses; even his guards refused to wear the new uniforms he had chosen for them. His cruelty to his wife appalled the English; because of her infidelity he imprisoned her for thirty-two years and she was never allowed to see her children; his eldest son hated him for this. He was even less welcome in Scotland where the nobility referred to him as that 'Wee German Lairdie' who should never have been crowned. After the failure of the 1715 Jacobite rebellion he ruthlessly put to death six Scottish nobles and struck down Lady Nithsdale when she pleaded for the life of her husband. George I's position was particularly precarious when the South Sea Company crashed in 1720; German fraud was suspected. In 1727 he died of a cerebral haemorrhage in Osnabrück in Hanover where he was buried.

George II, arrogant as a young man, was well educated and by the time he was crowned, in 1727 aged forty-three, he had a sound understanding of British politics. He was subtly dominated by his wife Queen Caroline who ignored his propensity for many mistresses. She and Prime Minister Walpole understood each other perfectly; he owed his survival to their friendship. George II treated his eldest son, Frederick, abominably — a Hanoverian trait. After ten years of kingship he began to detest the English ways and was heard to say: 'I am sick to death of all this foolish stuff and wish with all my heart that the devil may take all your bishops, and the devil take your Minister and the devil take your Parliament and the devil take the whole island provided I can get out of it and go to Hanover'. In fact he almost got his wish on receiving the news that Charles Edward Stuart had reached Derby during the '45 Rebellion. However, his favourite son, 'Butcher Cumberland', finally vanquished the Jacobites after their long trek back north to Culloden in 1746. George II was the last monarch to lead an army in battle — against the Spanish in 1739 and again in 1743 against the French. His death, on 25th October 1760, was sudden. He suffered from constipation and died in his toilet.

George III was the first Hanoverian to be born and educated in England. His reign coincided with a period of great change, much of it against his will. His government from 1763 to 1782 was an unmitigated mess. Even his boyhood friend Lord North referred to it as the 'choppings and changes'. George III was indecisive and excitable under pressure; he was weak and yet stubborn and although he tried to get rid of corruption he spent as much on bribes as his predecessor. He was intensely patriotic, religious, hard-working and, in the eyes of his eldest son, boring. He married the German Princess Charlotte of Mecklenberg-Strelitz; a marriage dictated by protocol which produced fifteen children. He relied heavily on the advice of the Earl of Bute after whose Premiership he disposed of four Prime ministers in rapid succession — Grenville, Rockingham, Pitt and the Duke of Grafton. Lord North's premiership pleased him and after ten years even North was discredited. The American colonies were lost in 1776 and Rockingham set about reducing the power of the throne.

George astonished the government by dismissing

the Fox-North alliance and choosing his own Ministers. He was delighted with his choice of the twenty-four year old Pitt who held power for twenty-one years and his sound advice gave the King a few good years. However the continual bitter criticism of his dissolute eldest son was a constant aggravation and he began to show signs of mental instability in 1788 but another twelve years were to pass before the Prince of Wales got his wish to become Regent. George III was now quite insane. For the next ten years he was nursed by the Queen and he died a sad and sorry figure on 29th January 1820. He had not even noticed that his wife had died two years before. (A more comprehensive biography of George III is given in Capital Walk 1, number 17 on page 63 and George IV is covered fully in Capital Walk 1, number 21 on page 74.)

William IV, the third son of George III, had no thoughts of kingship as a young man. He had served as a midshipman from the age of thirteen. He loved the navy; in fact 'Sailor Billy', as he was called, had hoped for a naval career. The navy however did not love him — his officers applied en-masse for a transfer on his promotion to the captaincy of a frigate. After the death, in 1818, of Princess Charlotte, George IV's only daughter, it became urgent to produce a royal heir and William married Princess Adelaide; he had already fathered ten illegitimate children by an actress, Mrs Jordan. His eccentricity seemed to increase with age; as High Admiral of England he raised his standard at Plymouth and defied the Admiralty by taking a squadron out to sea; he went to inordinate lengths to preserve his health in order to outlive the king and on receiving news of his death, on 26th June 1830, he could hardly conceal his delight. He was king aged sixty-four and quite unprepared for kingship. He swept through the streets of London doffing his hat to passers-by. His coronation was frugal in comparison to that of George IV, in fact his reign was one of economies verging on meanness. In 1831 Earl Grey asked him, at short notice, to dissolve Parliament so that he might be returned with a larger Whig majority to carry the new Reform Bill of 1832. His niece, Princess Victoria, was next in line and his main concern was that he might live until she reached the age of eighteen thus ensuring that her mother, whom he detested, should not become Regent.

He got his wish and died on 20th June 1837, one month after Victoria's eighteenth birthday.

Queen Victoria had the longest reign — almost two thirds of a century, and the greatest empire — one fifth of the globe. Her accession to the throne in 1837 ended the link with the House of Hanover. Britain was poised for expansion. At first she was advised by her Prime Minister and confidant Lord Melbourne who had little regard for reform or for the dreadful poverty throughout the country; she was quite unaware of the unrest until, in 1840, an attempt on her life made her realise her unpopularity. It was Prince Albert who gave her a social conscience; he virtually dragged her round the country to see her people. They were married in February 1840, she was very much in love but he was not trusted in Parliament. They had nine children; at first she was somewhat distant from them but she and Albert took a strong interest in their health and education, although Prince Edward was an incorrigible problem. Albert worked himself to exhaustion for the interests of the poor and died of typhoid in 1861. She was heartbroken and mourned for many years. Her seclusion from public life evoked criticism and she was surprised at the warmth of the welcome given to her when she eventually appeared in public for her golden jubilee (1887). When gold was discovered in Australia, two colonies were named after her — Victoria and Queensland. Prime Minister Disraeli made her Empress of India in 1857. In Africa diamond and gold discoveries brought thousands of colonists and Cecil Rhodes added to the vast land areas already taken under British protection. David Livingstone, in charting the Zambesi River, discovered the 5700ft/1737m-wide waterfalls which he named after her. By the time Mafeking was relieved in 1900 during the Boer War she was eighty and did not live to celebrate the end of the war in 1902. She died at Osborne on 22nd January 1901 aged eighty-two in the arms of her grandson, the Kaiser of Germany.

23 North and South St David Street

North and South St David's Street, at the west corners of St Andrew Square, were, according to Thomas Carlyle's autobiography *Jupiter*, named by David Hume and Miss Nancy Orde (daughter of Chief Baron Orde) who arranged that the name St David be painted on the cornerstone of Hume's house at the southwest corner of St Andrew Square. However the name has no connection with David Hume, it is simply a compliment to St David, the patron saint of Wales, according to Ainslie's plans of Edinburgh, 1790.

St David was a 6th century monk and bishop who is said to have inherited a monastery from his father in Henallan in Wales. He was born about the year 520AD and educated at Hen Vynyw after which he spent ten lonely and frugal years on an island where he studied the scriptures with Paulinus, the scribe.

David returned to the mainland and founded ten monasteries including Mynyw in Pembrokeshire (Dyfed) and Glastonbury. His life with the monks at Glastonbury was one of almost cruel and dedicated hard labour with a meagre diet of bread, vegetables and water. He continued his studies and dedicated himself to helping the poor. But this was not enough and he felt the need for greater physical sacrifice; he regularly immersed himself in freezing water and spent long periods on his knees in prayer.

At the Synod of Brevi in Cardiganshire his preaching was so inspiring it was said that he seemed to be elevated to a hill where a white dove appeared on his shoulder — religious art depicts him in this way. He was chosen by the Council of Brevi to be the Primate of Wales. His importance was exaggerated by a Welsh biographer in the 11th century who, in order to try to free the Welsh church from dependence upon Canterbury, made up the story that David had travelled to Jerusalem to receive episcopal consecration as Archbishop.

The cult of St David was approved in 1120 by Pope Callistus II when it was decreed that two pilgrimages to the shrine of St David would be equal to one pilgrimage to Rome. His first monastery at Mynyw, now the diocese of St David, is the title of the Catholic See. David travelled widely to establish over fifty monasteries throughout southern England. He advocated and inspired the Welsh monastic life of arduous self sacrifice through manual labour, absolute silence, rigorous fasting and total abstinence — only water was permitted; this gained him the name of 'Waterman'.

He died on 1st March 589AD, his dying words being 'keep the faith; observe exactly all the little things that you have learned from me'. His relics were translated firstly in 1131 and again in 1275 by Richard Carew, the Bishop of St David's, who rebuilt the cathedral almost entirely from offerings at the shrine. Two English Kings made the pilgrimage to St David's, William I and Henry II.

Many Welshmen wear the daffodil on 1st March — St David's day. There is no credible explanation for this except perhaps that the Welsh spelling of David is Dafydd — the nearest phonetic sound to daffodil which led to its recognition as the emblem of Wales. The leek is another national emblem of Wales which, according to legend, was worn by Welshmen, at the instigation of St David, and brought them victory at the Battle of Heathfield in 633AD.

24 Saint Andrew Square

At the east end of George Street we enter Saint Andrew Square, the north side of which has most of its original houses built in 1770-72 but considerably altered with new windows, doorpieces and porches — a porch, pediment and balustrade at No.26, an Ionic porch at No.25, a Roman Doric porch at No.24 and No.23 with its pedimented porch has a magnificent Italian Renaissance facade. No.21, the birthplace of Henry P. Brougham (1778-1868), was refaced in ashlar with

ST ANDREW SQUARE WHICH DATES FROM THE LATE 18TH CENTURY

a Doric porch and entablature and No.22, also in ashlar, has a Greek Corinthian porch. In the centre of the east side the grand Georgian house, No. 36, set back from the line of houses was designed for Sir Laurence Dundas in 1771 by Sir William Chambers. It became the Excise Office in 1794 when the gilt Royal Arms (the pre-Union with Ireland version) were added to its central pediment which is supported by Corinthian pilasters. The house is now the registered office of the Royal Bank of Scotland plc., and in its garden is the statue of the 4th Earl of Hopetoun. The statue of Henry Dundas, the Melville monument, is in the central garden of the Square.

Saint Andrew Square commemorates the patron saint of Scotland (and of Romania, Greece and Russia). As Christ was crucified so too was St Andrew but on a diagonal cross (the crux decussata); he believed himself unworthy of the same manner of death as his master. He was one of the twelve apostles and he brought his brother, Simon Peter, to meet Christ. Andrew spread the gospel of Christianity preaching in Greece and throughout Asia minor. He is said to have travelled as far north as Kiev in Russia where a church was founded in his name.

He never actually visited Scotland but it is recorded that St Regulus (St Rule) travelled from Patras (now Patrai in Greece) to Muckross or Kilrimont (now St Andrews) where he was shipwrecked, in 347AD. He brought relics of St Andrew from the east having had a vision that the Eastern Roman Emperor Constantius intended to take the relics to Constantinople; St Regulus forestalled him by taking an arm bone, three fingers and a tooth to Scotland. However a later version states that the French Crusaders, having sacked Constantinople in 1204, took some of St Andrew's relics to Western Europe and Cardinal Capua took the body of St Andrew to Amalfi in Italy after the fall of Constantinople.

In 735AD, at the Battle of Athelstaneford, it was said that Angus MacFergus, King of the Picts, had a vision of a white cross in the blue sky and that he heard the voice of St Andrew which so inspired him to victory that the Saltire was, from that day adopted as the symbol of good fortune and King Angus took it as the national emblem. The Scottish soldiers of the 14th century were ordered to wear the saltire on their armour to reaffirm their belief in the righteousness of their cause, to bring them luck, to discourage their enemy and to be recognisable to each other.

It was from about 735AD until 1559 that the relics of St Andrew were held in great respect by Scots. Cardinal Beaton was said to have used one of the relics, an arm bone, as a symbol of protection in his plea for help against Henry VIII's troops, but to no avail; he was murdered by conspirators in 1546. In June of 1559 the interior of St Andrews Cathedral and the chapel containing the relics were destroyed by a ransacking mob of Reformers who had been inflamed by the preaching of John Knox against the Church of Rome.

St Andrews became the spiritual centre of Scotland, visited by many pilgrims. A hospice was built to shelter them and in the Cathedral of St Andrews, Robert the Bruce prayed in gratitude for his victory over the English at Bannockburn on 24th June 1314.

In 1879 the Marquess of Bute donated a silver gilt shrine to St Mary's Metropolitan Cathedral in York Place to accommodate the newly-gifted shoulder blade of St Andrew from the Archbishop of Amalfi. Ninety years later, in 1969, a second relic was given to the newly created Cardinal Gray by Pope Paul VI and today the two relics are contained in special reliquaries.

St Andrew was crucified on the orders of the Roman Governor in Achaia in 69AD. His bones were taken to Byzantium, the Eastern capital of the Roman Empire but in 1462 his head was taken to St Peters in Rome, arriving with great ceremony in Holy Week. It was returned by Pope Paul VI to the Greek Orthodox Church in Patras on 23rd September 1964. The last resting place of the body of St Andrew is in St Andrews Cathedral in Amalfi near Naples.

25 Melville Monument

In the central garden of Saint Andrew Square stands the 121ft/37m high Doric column and the 14ft/4.2m high statue of the Rt. Hon Henry Dundas, 1st Viscount Melville. The monument, by William Burn, was modelled on the column of Trajan in Rome and the statue was sculpted by Robert Forrest. The monument was paid for by officers and men of the Royal Navy in 1921.

Henry Dundas was the most powerful and influential man in Scotland in his day; he was a despot and 'absolute dictator'. He was born in Bishop's Close in the High Street in 1742. His father was Robert Dundas of Arniston, Lord President of the Court of Session, his grandfather and great grandfather were also Lord Presidents. Henry was educated at the High School and at the University of Edinburgh where he studied law. He became an advocate at the age of twenty-one, he was elected MP for Midlothian in 1774 and a year later he was appointed Lord Advocate which he held until 1783.

For the twenty-three years between 1782 and 1805 Henry Dundas virtually managed the affairs of Scotland as 'King Harry the ninth'. Lord Cockburn's *Memorials of His Time* described him thus:

> … an Edinburgh man, and well calculated by talent and manner to make despotism popular, was absolute dictator of Scotland, and of extinguishing opposition beyond what were ever exercised in modern times by one person in any portion of the empire.

Under his smiling, friendly exterior were hidden

many intrigues and ambitions. Four generations of the Dundas family had held almost absolute authority holding the offices of Judge, Solicitor-General, Lord Advocate and Lord President of the Court of Session in Scotland. At that time there were forty-five Parliamentary seats — thirty County seats with only 2662 voters and fifteen seats chosen by the Royal Burghs and well known to be self-perpetuating. In 1790, such was the influence of Dundas, he delivered thirty-four of these Scottish seats to his Prime Minister, William Pitt. Dundas obtained these voters by promising favours and appointments in high places, often in India.

In 1791 Dundas was appointed Home Secretary; then followed 'Pitt's reign of terror', 1793-94. The repression continued for another thirty years, Pitt being well supported by the Dundas family who in turn had the juducial support of the fearsome Lord Braxfield — the 'Judge Jeffreys' of Scotland, who during the political trials of 1793-94, simply deported or hanged opponents. The brilliant young advocate Thomas Muir was one of those unfortunates to be sentenced for sedition even though the prosecution could not prove the charge; he was sentenced for fourteen years' transportation. The Prosecuter was Robert Dundas, nephew of Henry Dundas.

Henry Dundas had married into title and considerable wealth but in his busy and ambitious Parliamentary career he woefully neglected his young wife who, during his many absences from home, left him for a younger and more attentive man, Captain Faukener.

By 1796 opposition was growing against Dundas's unseemly and overt power. Henry Erskine, who led the opposition, found himself deposed from the Deanship of the Faculty of Advocates. This was serious because no-one was held in greater esteem than the popular Henry Erskine. In 1801 Dundas resigned his Ministerial post with Prime Minister Pitt over the 'Irish problem'. The following year Dundas was elevated to Viscount Melville and Baron of Dunira.

While serving as Secretary of War in 1805 he was accused of using Navy funds to purchase shares in the East India Company; as Treasurer of the Navy he had controlled the finances in his own way for over forty years without question; his paymaster, Alexander Trotter of Dreghorn, had made a tidy profit from their arrangements in which he habitually took cheques for 'storage' in his account in his cousin Coutt's bank. Dundas had allegedly borrowed money from this source. He was impeached of 'gross malversation and breach of duty'. His two-week trial in the House of Lords acquitted him. His friends, including Sir Walter Scott, were overjoyed and a public dinner was given in his honour by the Edinburgh Town Council on 27th June 1806. His only fault was described as carelessness rather than acquisitiveness but that was the end of the Pitt-Dundas era and he retired to his estate of Dunira near Comrie in Perthshire.

He died in May 1811 on the day before the funeral of his friend and neighbour, Lord President Robert Blair, whose sudden death undoubtedly affected Lord Melville. It is said that his last act was to write a letter to the Government pleading for some provision for Blair's family. The two great men lay dead next door to each other in their adjacent houses in George Square. Lord Melville was buried at Lasswade.

26 Earl of Hopetoun Monument
No.36 St Andrew Square

The Hopetoun Monument is prominent in the manicured garden of the registered office of the Royal Bank of Scotland, originally a grand Georgian House built for Sir Laurence Dundas in 1771. The monument, erected in 1834, is that of the 4th Earl of Hopetoun in the dress of a Roman general standing by his horse. The bronze statue was designed by sculptor Thomas Campbell in 1824-29 and was originally intended for Charlotte Square. He was a brave soldier under Abercrombie, a heroic general under Wellington and a governor of the Royal Bank of Scotland — the site in the garden of the bank was therefore deemed appropriate.

The family seat is Hopetoun House near Queensferry built for Charles Hope, the 1st Earl of Hopetoun, in 1699 who commissioned Sir William Bruce to build it. However it was considerably altered by the 2nd Earl when William Adam's extensions were added in 1721; Adam's sons Robert and John designed the interior in 1767. A visit to Hopetoun House is an architectural and historical experience of the highest order.

The 4th Earl of Hopetoun, Sir John Hope, was born on 17th August 1765 at Hopetoun House; his father, also John Hope, married three times and it was by his second wife, Jane Oliphant, that John was born. He succeeded to the title as the 4th Earl in 1816 on the death of his step brother James, the 3rd Earl.

He was educated by tutors at Hopetoun House and he started his army career, aged eighteen, as a cornet (sub-lieutenant) in the 10th Light Dragoons. He rose steadily through the ranks to attain the rank of lieutenant-colonel of the 25th Foot within nine years and he was returned as MP for Linlithgowshire during this period.

At the start of the war with France in 1793 he was stationed at Plymouth for two years after which he was sent to the West Indies in command of ten companies but illness forced him home. He returned a year later as adjutant-general under Sir Ralph Abercrombie who commended him several times for bravery under fire at the destruction of French and Spanish strongholds. He served in Holland (1799), the Mediterranean (1800) and Egypt (1801) where he was badly wounded at the Battle of Aboukir on 21st March and where his general, Abercrombie, was tragically killed by a stray bullet. Hope had commanded two of the most distinguished regiments of the British Army — the 28th Foot and the 42nd Highlanders and he was deputed to arrange the surrender of the French in 1802 after the Peace of Amiens. But that year was disastrous for him; not only did he suffer severely from his wounds but his wife, Elizabeth Hope-Vere died.

In 1803 he married Louisa Dorothea, daughter of Sir John Wedderburn; they had eleven children. He was promoted to major-general in command of a brigade on the east coast of England to defend against threatened invasion. Two years later he was appointed Lieutenant-General of Portsmouth but he was anxious to join the expedition to Hanover and he resigned his appointment to do so. In 1808, now a lieutenant-general, Hope was sent to Sweden and then to Portugal under Sir John Moore, the great Glasgow general. Hope commanded a division and linked up with Moore at Salamanca but the odds were too great against them and they were forced to retreat over 250 miles of snow-covered hills and mountains to Corunna where Sir John Moore was killed on the point of victory. During the embarkation to England Hope rode through every street in Corunna to ensure the safety of his men; this act of determined, brave compassion earned him the thanks of Parliament and a Knighthood of the Order of the Bath from George III.

Hope was appointed commander of the forces in Ireland in 1812 and the following year he succeeded Sir Thomas Graham (later Lord Lynedoch) in the Peninsular army to command a division under Wellington at the Battles of Nivelle and Nive where he was wounded. Wellington thus described him:

> I have long entertained the highest opinion of Sir John Hope, … but every day more convinces me of his worth. We shall lose him if he continues to expose himself as he did during the last three days. Indeed his escape was wonderful. His coat and hat were shot through in many places, besides the wound in his leg. He places himself among the sharpshooters, without sheltering himself as they do … he is the ablest man in the Peninsular army.

In February 1814 Hope blockaded Bayonne on the south-east coast of France with stubbornness and skill until the end of the war. He had his horse shot from under him and, wounded again, he was captured but soon released. After Wellington's magnificent victory at Waterloo in 1815, which marked the total and final defeat of Napoleon, Hope was raised to the peerage as Baron Niddry of Niddry Castle in Linlithgowshire.

In 1816 he succeeded his half brother as the 4th Earl of Hopetoun and he became a full general in 1819. He was delighted and honoured to be appointed Colonel of the famous 42nd Highlanders. He was Lord Lieutenant of Linlithgowshire, a governor of the Royal Bank of Scotland and, as Captain of the Royal Company of Archers, the King's Bodyguard in Scotland, he attended George IV during his visit to Scotland in 1822. He entertained the king at Hopetoun House to celebrate the first Royal visit since that of Charles II in 1650.

His death was sudden — it occurred during a visit to Paris ten days after his fifty-eighth birthday on 27th August 1823. He was mourned not only for his integrity, his strong commonsense but as a courageous soldier who was well liked both in the army and as a civilian. He was succeeded by his eldest of nine sons.

The last stop of this tour walk is appropriately inside the Georgian house which is the head office of the Royal Bank of Scotland — inlaid on the floor of the entrance hall there is a small brass plaque which is the datum point of James Craig's plan of the New Town.

This beautiful building was built four years before Craig's plan was drawn. It was built between 1772-74 for Laurence Dundas MP for the City who died in 1781 and the house was sold seven years later to the Government. It became the Exise Office in 1794 replacing that at Chessel's Court in the Old Town (where Deacon Brodie perpetrated his last burglary in 1788) The pre-1801 Royal Coat-of-Arms was added to the pediment at that time. In 1825 the house finally changed hands to become the Royal Bank of Scotland and Archibald Elliott (the son) was commissioned to design the internal decorations and to add a porch in 1828. Further changes were made in 1836 by William Burn who designed the stairhall which became the vestibule in 1857 by John Dick Peddie when he added the magnificent telling-hall with its 120-starred dome.

Capital Walk 2

1 Scottish National Portrait Gallery
2 Queen Street
3 Abercrombie Place
4 Dundas Street
5 Heriot Row
6 Howe Street
7 Gloucester Lane
8 Moray Place

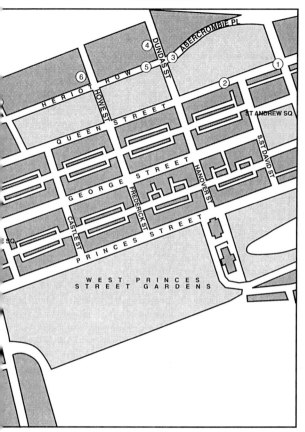

9   Randolph Crescent
10 Queensferry Street
11 Melville Street and Statue
12 Walker Street
13 Rothesay Place
14 Palmerston Place
15 Glencairn Crescent
16 Eglinton Crescent
17 Grosvenor Crescent
18 Lansdowne Crescent
19 Atholl Crescent
20 Gladstone Memorial

1   Scottish National Portrait Gallery

Start at the Scottish National Portrait Gallery, the entrance to which is in Queen Street. If you would like to see portraits of some 'Great Scots' it is well worth visiting this Venetian-French Gothic gallery and museum which was a gift to the nation by J.R. Finlay who owned The Scotsman. It was designed by R. Rowand Anderson and built in 1885-90 for the sum of £50,000.

2   Queen Street

Overlooking the River Forth to the hills of Fife, this street has some of the New Town's most prestigious houses, most of which are in their original state. It is named after Queen Chàrlotte (1744-1818) who was married to George III in 1761 on the night she landed in England. She had fifteen children and was — perhaps not surprisingly — humourless; life at court was extremely dull. She nursed her husband after he became insane from 1810 and died of overwork two years before him in 1818.

3   Abercrombie Place

Leaving Queen Street the first turning to the right leads to the junction of Abercrombie Place, Dundas Street and Heriot Row. Abercrombie Place, designed by Robert Reid in 1805, overlooks Queen Street Gardens. It was the first crescent-shaped street in Edinburgh and was named after Sir Ralph Abercrombie (1734-1801) the army commander who served in the Seven Years War (1754-63) which incidentally lasted for nine!. In the Revolutionary and Napoleonic Wars with France (1793-1815) he was killed at the Battle of Aboukir in Egypt in 1801.

4   Dundas Street

Building started in 1807, the street being named after Henry Dundas, 1st Viscount Melville (1742-1811). His power over Scotland was almost a family tradition —

his brother, father, grandfather, and great-grandfather all held positions of power. Henry Dundas was Solicitor-General for Scotland, MP for Midlothian and Lord Advocate under Prime Ministers North and Rockingham. In Parliament he was President of the Board of Control in 1784 under Pitt to whom he 'gifted' almost three-quarters of the Scottish Parliamentary seats through despotism and bribery. His impeachment for 'gross malversation' when he was Treasurer of the Navy was found to be without foundation (he had allegedly borrowed money to buy shares) and his friends including Sir Walter Scott were overjoyed. A celebration dinner was given by Edinburgh Town Council in 1806 in his honour. He retired to his estate in Dunira in Perthshire where he died five years later.

5   Heriot Row

Designed by Robert Reid in 1802, the street originally had two-storey houses but in 1864 David Bryce added a third at its west end. It is named after George Heriot (1563-1642) who was given the name 'Jingling Geordie' by Sir Walter Scott. He was the favourite jeweller of Queen Anne and was appointed Goldsmith to the King. He left a huge fortune and endowed George Heriot's School and the Heriot Trust and partially financed the Heriot-Watt University. No.17 Heriot Row was the residence of Thomas Stevenson father of Robert Louis Stevenson (1850-94) the world-famous novelist who wrote *Kidnapped*, *Treasure Island*, *Dr Jekyll and Mr Hyde* and many other favourites. He suffered from tuberculosis and eventually died in his beloved Samoa in the Pacific.

6   Howe Street

Howe Street, with its stepped tenements leading downhill to Royal Circus, is named after Richard, 1st Earl Howe (1726-99), a famous British Admiral who served in the Seven Years War. He was a Lord of the Admiralty and Treasurer of the Navy, Commander-in-Chief in the Channel, Admiral of the Blue, First Lord of the Admiralty and as Admiral of the White he out-manoeuvered the French fleet 300 miles west of Ushant — the 'Glorious 1st of June' 1790. He was hailed as a great hero.

7   Gloucester Lane

At the end of Heriot Row, Gloucester Lane leads to Gloucester Place; the latter was built in 1850 and re-named (from Church Street) in 1966. Gloucester Lane and Place were named after William Frederick, 2nd Duke of Gloucester and Edinburgh (1776-1834). He gained an MA at Cambridge, an LL.D and was elected a Fellow of the Royal Society (FRS); he was a Field Marshal in 1816 and after his retirement gave most of his income to charity.

8   Moray Place

Entry to Moray Place is via Darnaway Street. Moray Place was designed by James Gillespie Graham and is duodecagonal (twelve-sided) in shape; it is one of the most beautiful and prestigious squares in Edinburgh and is named after the Earl of Moray (1531-70) on whose estate it is built. The radiating streets off Moray Place are Darnaway Street and Forres Street which take their names from Darnaway Castle near Forres, one of the seats of the Earl of Moray.

Moray Place and Great Stuart Street are named after the Earl of Moray who was the illegitimate son of James V of Scotland. Mary Queen of Scots created him Earl of Moray and Earl of Mar; he was appointed Regent after Mary's escape from Lochleven, defeating her army at Langside in 1568. He brought a long-awaited peace to Scotland and came to be called the 'Good Regent' but he was assassinated in 1570. From Great Stuart Street we enter Ainslie Place which is named after the 10th Earl of Moray's second wife, Margaret Jane, daughter of Sir Philip Ainslie of Pilton.

9 Randolph Crescent

From Ainslie Place to Great Stuart Street we now enter the centre of Randolph Crescent each side of which runs into Queensferry Street. Built in the Moray Estate in the 1820s, its houses have attractive arched entrances and Roman Doric pilasters. It is named after Sir Thomas Randolph who was created Earl of Moray by his uncle, King Robert the Bruce. He was one of Bruce's most loyal supporters from 1308. He daringly captured Edinburgh Castle from the English and fought under Bruce at the Battle of Bannockburn — Scottish history marks him as one of the great heroes.

10 Queensferry Street

Leaving Randolph Crescent from its left hand north section, Queensferry Street, the main road, is named after Queen Margaret (c1045-1093) wife of Malcolm III. She brought the Church of Rome to Scotland, replacing the Celtic Church, and she literally washed the feet of the poor. Pilgrims to St Andrews shrine had their journey made easier by her kindness in establishing a ferry for them across the River Forth — hence the name Queensferry. She had a premonition of her husband's death while he was away in battle against the English. She died shortly afterwards and her enshrouded body was taken secretly from St Margaret's Chapel in Edinburgh Castle to her church in Dunfermline. She was canonised in 1251 by Pope Innocent IV.

11 Melville Street and Statue

Crossing over the busy Queensferry Street we reach Melville Street in the Western New Town. Melville Street was designed by Robert Brown in 1814 as the main street of the Walker development, so named because it was built on Sir Patrick Walker's land. Melville Street is named after Henry Dundas, 1st Viscount Melville.

Half way along Melville Street is Melville Crescent which is a square set diagonally with the statue of Robert Dundas, 2nd Viscount Melville (1771-1851), by

John Steell (1857) in its centre. He continued the family tradition of 'managing' the affairs of Scotland.

12 Walker Street

Leading to Drumsheugh Gardens, this street is named after Sir Patrick Walker (1777-1837) who owned the estates of Coates and Drumsheugh. He was an advocate who was rich enough to avoid the necessity of actually practising law! He was Heritable Usher of the White Rod — a ceremonial post and he was knighted for his services far beyond the requirements of the title. At the procession of George IV in 1822 in Edinburgh he was conspicuously resplendent in gold and scarlet on his white charger.

13 Rothesay Place

Rothesay Place and Terrace were designed from 1872 and named after the Duke of Rothesay, the Scottish title of the Prince of Wales, who became Edward VII (1841-1910) whose mother, Queen Victoria, blamed him for the death of his father, Prince Albert. As Prince of Wales he was denied access to state papers and not given any responsibility except to unveil statues etc. In his self-indulgence he consumed huge meals, enjoyed sport, gambling and women. He was fifty-nine when he became king and his tour of Europe gave him the name 'Edward the Peacemaker'. He died in the middle of a constitutional crisis — Lloyd George's 'War Budget' — the war against poverty.

14 Palmerston Place

This place is named after Henry John Temple Palmerston, 3rd Viscount (1784-1865) who was Foreign Secretary in 1830 and 1846, Prime Minister in 1855, 1857 and 1859, supporter of the Reform Bill of 1832 and heartily disliked by Queen Victoria. He was Prime Minister of the nation rather than of a political party. His interfering ways in foreign affairs gave him the deserved reputation of 'Firebrand Palmerston'.

15 Glencairn Crescent

This is one of a pair of crescents on the west side of Palmerston Place. It was built by John Steele in 1873-79 and designed by John Chesser. The Earls of Glencairn are descended from Cunningham of Ayrshire. The title died in 1791 with the 14th Earl who was a valued patron of Robert Burns. Glencairn Crescent is probably named ater the Countess of Glencairn who feued the land of West Coates in 1792; she died in 1801.

16 Eglinton Crescent

Designed by John Chesser and built in 1875-80, the crescent is named after Hugh Montgomerie, 12th Earl of Eglinton (1739-1819), who was every ounce a feudal baron. He enjoyed magnificence and grandeur and rebuilt the castle of Eglinton in grand, castellated style. He built the harbour at Ardrossan intending it to be the port of Glasgow but the necessary canal was too expensive. He was an accomplished musician, MP for Ayrshire, a representative peer of Scotland and a Knight of the Thistle.

17 Grosvenor Crescent

Immediately opposite St Mary's Cathedral and designed by John Chesser in 1869, the cathedral was built from the legacy of the Walker sisters, the heiresses of Patrick Walker. It was designed by G. Gilbert Scott in 1872 and finished by his two sons, John and Charles, in 1917. Grosvenor Crescent is named after the Earls of Grosvenor; the family arrived in England with William the Conqueror in 1066. Their Baronetcy dates from 1622, the Earldom from 1784 and the Dukedom of Westminister from 1874. The 1st Duke followed the passion of his father — horse racing; he had four Derby winners. The present duke is considered to be the richest landowner in Britain.

18 Lansdowne Crescent

Opposite Grosvenor Crescent and designed by Robert Matheson in 1865; it is named after Henry Charles Keith Petty-Fitzmaurice, the 5th Earl of Lansdowne (1845-1927) who was Governor-General of Canada in 1883, Viceroy of India in 1888 and Secretary of State for War and Foreign Secretary in consecutive unionist administrations. In 1905 he became Conservative leader of the opposition and he was a member of the Coalition Cabinet at the outbreak of war in 1914 but he was ousted for the publication of his Peace Accommodation in 1917. At the end of Palmerston Place we turn left (westwards) along West Maitland Street (named after Alexander Charles Maitland of Cliftonhall who opened the way to Charlotte Square and Princes Street in 1805).

19 Atholl Crescent

Atholl Crescent, opposite Coates Crescent with its trellis balconies, has ten central Ionic pilasters and another five at each end of the Crescent; it was designed by Thomas Bonnar in 1825 and named after the Dukes of Atholl whose ancestral home is Blair Castle in Blair Atholl. The 1st Duke, John Murray, was vehemently against the Union of Parliaments in 1707 and the family supported the Jacobite rebellions of 1715 and 1745. Coates Crescent, opposite Atholl Crescent, was the first to be built in the western New Town (1813); it is split by Walker Street and is named after the owner of the estates of Coates and Drumsheugh, Sir Patrick Walker (1777-1837).

20 Gladstone Memorial

This statue in the garden of Coates Crescent, was sculpted by J.Pittendrigh MacGillivray in 1902 and commemorates William Ewart Gladstone (1809-98), Prime Minister from 1868 until 1874, 1880 to 1885 and 1892 to 1898 — a great statesman whose legacy of successful legislation is probably unsurpassed in the history of politics.

Historical biographies

1 Scottish National Portrait Gallery

This tour walk starts at the corner of North St Andrew Street and Queen Street at the Scottish National Portrait Gallery — a Venetian-French Gothic masterpiece of orange-red sandstone. It was built in 1885-90 and designed by R. Rowand Anderson as a portrait gallery and a museum. It was made possible by the munificence of J.R. Finlay, the owner of The Scotsman who gave £50,000 for its completion. At the time of writing there is, unbelievably, an agonising controversy as to the future location of its paintings with the new Gallery of Scottish Art being proposed for Glasgow.

The Scottish National Portrait Gallery and museum is the home of 2364 historical and contemporary portraits and museum pieces. To learn of those who shaped Scotland's history, indeed of those who shaped world history over a period of four hundred years, visits to this gallery and museum are essential. Whatever one's interest — whether it be art (in portraiture or sculpture), science, history, medicine, literature, law, politics — this gallery will more than simply whet the appetite.

The interior is grand with its two-storey central hall, red sandstone columns and corner piers, the capitals of which were carved by students of the Edinburgh College of Art. The frieze over the arcade is a history lesson of saints and soldiers, kings and queens, dukes and earls, poets, philosophers and politicians, jurists, explorers and discoverers, scientists, engineers and writers. They date from Roman times to the nineteenth century. The great library of the Society of Antiquaries of Scotland is to be found on the second floor and the stained-glass window on the stair to the library has medallion portraits of some famous antiquaries. Among the museum exhibits is the famous 'Maiden', Scotland's guillotine which has severed many a famous and infamous head in its time.

On the outside, around the building are sculptures of historical figures which are set in niches in octagonal turrets. The central niche at the east end contains a group of three by W. Birnie Rhind:

William Maitland of Lethington (c1528-73), Secretary of State to the Queen Regent, Mary of Guise; Mary Queen of Scots (1542-87), who was forced to abdicate in 1567. She was beheaded in England in 1587 and Bishop Leslie (1527-96), Bishop of Ross and a strong supporter of Mary Queen of Scots. The other sculptures include:

Admiral Adam Duncan, Viscount Camperdown (1731-1804), the victor over the Dutch at Camperdown in 1795; David Hume (1711-76), the great Scottish philosopher and historian; Adam Smith (1723-90), the father of modern economics and author of the *Wealth of Nations*; James Hutton (1726-97), the father of modern geology; Sir Henry Raeburn (1756-1823), portrait painter to George III; Lord John Napier (1550-1617), the inventor of logarithms; John Barbour (c1320-95), the father of Scottish poetry and historical writing; William Dunbar (c1460-c1520), the Scottish poet, satirist and writer of hymns; Gavin Douglas (1474-1522), poet Bishop of Dunkeld and Dean of St Giles; Sir David Lyndsay (c1468-1555), Lyon King-of Arms in 1538; John Knox (c1505-72), Scotland's leading Reformer of the Church; George Buchanan (1506-82), tutor to Mary Queen of Scots and to her son James VI; Cardinal Beaton (c1494-1546), Archbishop of St Andrews and persecutor of Protestants; John Campbell, 2nd Duke of Argyll (1678-1743), who controlled Scottish affairs during the reign of George I; Alexander III (1241-86), King of Scotland from 1249-86; James I (1394-1437), who reigned from 1406 to 1437 and provided a uniform legal system for rich and poor; James V (1512-42), who reigned from 1513-42, instituted the College of Justice and was father of Mary Queen of Scots; James Stuart, Earl of Moray (1531-70), the 'Good Regent'; James VI (I of England) (1566-1625), inherited the throne of England in 1603 (the Union of the Crowns); Malcolm Canmore (c1035-93), became king after Macbeth's death in 1057 and married Queen Margaret in 1069; Queen Margaret (1045-93), married Malcolm III and brought Roman Catholicism to Scotland. She was canonised in 1251.

Finally, perhaps Scotland's most famous sons, Robert the Bruce (1274-1329), who liberated the nation from English domination after the Battle of Bannockburn in 1314 and Sir William Wallace (c1274-1035), Guardian of Scotland and the man who prepared the way for the independence of Scotland.

2 *Queen Street*

Queen Street is the northern extremity of James Craig's medal-winning plan of the first New Town and, like Princes Street, is one-sided with splendid views over its gardens to the River Forth and beyond to Fife. Walking westwards from the Scottish National Portrait Gallery the five-bay villa at No.8 was designed for the English judge Baron Orde by Robert Adam in 1770. It is now the office of Scottish Council for Postgraduate Medical Education. Nos.9&10 are the neo-classical Royal College of Physicians. Its two-storey porch was designed by Thomas Hamilton in 1844.

Queen Street is named after Queen Charlotte, as is Charlotte Square; a biography of Queen Charlotte appears in Capital Walk 1, number 15 on page 56.

3 *Abercrombie Place*

Having left Queen Street and walked northwards down Queen Street Gardens East to the junction of Abercrombie Place on right hand side with Dundas Street ahead and Heriot Row to the left, we have reached some of the finest houses of the northern New Town. No.17 Abercrombie Place was the first Edinburgh address of the eminent architect William H. Playfair (see Capital Walk 1, number 9 on page 41).

Abercrombie Place was designed by Robert Reid in 1805. This crescent-shaped street, the first of its kind in Edinburgh, is named after Sir Ralph Abercrombie (1734-1801) the army commander. Ralph Abercrombie was born in 1734 in Tullibody, just north of Alloa in Clackmannanshire. He was educated at Rugby and studied law at the universities of Edinburgh and Leipzig. He became much more interested in the military and, aged twenty-two he gained a commission in the Dragoon Guards. He was involved in many victories during his service in the Seven Years War (1754-1763) in which Britain, allied with Frederick the Great of Prussia, fought against France, Austria and Russia. Abercrombie took every opportunity to study the military genius of Frederick the Great and was promoted to the rank of Colonel in an Irish regiment. It was quite obvious that Abercrombie's excellent army service

ABERCROMBIE PLACE — EDINBURGH'S FIRST CRESCENT-SHAPED STREET

would lead to greater promotion but he was opposed to George III's policy in America and he retired from active service in 1775.

He was elected M.P. for Clackmannanshire until 1780. However, as soon as the French declared war, he quickly re-enlisted to serve in Holland under the Duke of York in 1793. In 1796-7 in the West Indies he captured St Lucia and almost all of the remaining islands including Spanish Trinidad and Dutch Demerera in a brilliant campaign. As a Brigadier, under the Duke of York, Abercrombie covered the British retreat in the disastrous Dutch expedition of 1799. His military strategy in averting disaster earned him a Knighthood of the Order of the Bath.

Whilst Abercrombie was in command during the Irish rebellion in 1798 he tried to gain the confidence of the Irish by withholding the involvement of his troops from local disturbances. Again, however, he found himself in disagreement with the British Government which demanded a much tougher approach and he was forced to resign his commission pronouncing on the state of the Irish army as, 'licentious which rendered it formidable to everyone but the enemy'. The arrest of the leaders of the United Irishmen left them in chaos; the plot to take Dublin was thwarted and the rebellion defeated. He was appointed Commander of the Army in Scotland and afterwards was sent to Holland for the second time; the Anglo-Russian expedition, again a failure for the British.

His last campaign was in Egypt, on 21st March 1801, where he successfully routed the French. His landing at Aboukir Bay with 14,000 men on 8th March was a complete success in spite of very tough resistance and heavy fire; this was hailed as the greatest success of the war, but in an unexpected retaliatory attack by the French a stray bullet wounded him. However, he managed to hide the fact until assured of victory. He then fell from his horse through loss of blood and died seven days later on board the Admiral's flagship. The French lost 3000 men and the British 1200. General Sir Ralph Abercrombie was buried at the castle of St. Elmo in Valetta on the island of Malta. His title, Baron Abercrombie, was conferred on his widow and enjoyed by his son.

4 Dundas Street

The building of Dundas Street was started in 1808 following complaints from the feuars of Heriot Row and Northumberland Street who had been promised the roadway to Hanover Street on taking up their feus. The stepped tenements and pilastered Georgian shops of Dundas Street thus link Hanover Street to Canonmills.

This street was named after Henry Dundas, 1st Viscount of Melville. His biography appears in Capital Walk 1, number 25 on page 86.

5 Heriot Row

Heriot Row was built between 1803 and 1808; its east side was designed by Robert Reid in 1802 and its west terrace was altered by David Bryce in 1864 when he added a storey between the pavilions. One of its most famous residents was Robert Louis Stevenson who was brought up in No.17. The street, however, is named after George Heriot, an exceedingly wealthy goldsmith whose jewellery was so much in demand that James VI appointed him Jeweller to the King. George Heriot's School and Heriot-Watt University bear his name. Heriot left a fortune to endow George Heriot's School where his statue stands in the north entrance tower. Heriot-Watt University received its Royal Assent as a college on 12th August 1885 and its Royal Charter as a university on 31st January 1966. In 1969 it vacated Chambers Street for a new campus at Riccarton to the west of the city.

George Heriot became exceedingly rich during the reign of James VI. Heriot's house in the Old Fishmarket Close was a short walk to his shop (one of the luckenbooths around St Giles) where he started his business as a goldsmith in 1586. For a wedding present his father, who was one of the Heriots of Trabroun in East Lothian, set him up in business with the 'necessaries to ane buith' plus 1500 Scots merks, about £80,000 today!. His seven foot square booth was fully equipped with bellows, crucibles and tools for the art of goldsmithing. His father was a prosperous goldsmith and had given his son, from an early age, a thorough training in the art of making exquisite jewellery. His artistry was soon in demand and he was admitted a member of the Incorporation of Edinburgh Goldsmiths on 28th May 1588.

Born on 15th June 1563, George Heriot was one of that rare breed of men who combined skilful excellence, business acumen with a pleasing, generous personality. His jewellery and his polite eloquence caught the eye and the ear of King James and his Queen, Anne of Denmark. She had very expensive tastes and George Heriot received many orders from her and through her Royal patronage. She delighted in his workmanship; the Royal jewels were the envy of the court and in July 1597 Heriot was appointed Goldsmith for life to Queen

Anne. The king also found a trustworthy confidant in George Heriot and his appointment as 'Jeweller to the King' was announced from the Mercat Cross in April 1601. His future was assured; 'Jinglin' Geordie', as Sir Walter Scott nicknamed him, had arrived at Court.

In the ten years before the Union of the Crowns in 1603, it was estimated that Queen Anne had ordered £50,000 worth of jewellery (about £50 million today). George Heriot became very rich, so rich that he became the money-lender who virtually financed the Court. He lent money to the King and Queen who allowed him to pawn their jewellery deposited as security. On one occasion he held the title deeds of the Royal Chapel of Stirling as security on loans to the King and Queen. He was canny, discreet and not in the least demanding. Such was the King's confidence in Heriot as a trusted friend, he allotted him an apartment at

No 17 Heriot Row where Robert louis Stevenson lived

Holyroodhouse and appointed him to membership of a syndicate commissioned to issue a new Scottish currency.

In his *Old and New Edinburgh*, Grant relates the story of Heriot's visit to the Royal apartments at Holyroodhouse where he found the king sitting by a pleasant fire of sweet-smelling wood. Heriot remarked that he could show him an even more pleasing fire at his shop. The king promised to visit him and, on arrival at Heriot's tiny shop, found an ordinary fire.

'Is this the fire? the King asked.

'Let me put some fuel on it, your Majesty.'

Heriot then produced a bond for £2000 from his desk which was part of the King's debt. Heriot threw it on the fire.

'Now, is this not a more expensive fire?' Heriot mused.

When James VI left Edinburgh in the spring of 1603 to succeed Elizabeth I to become James I of England, Heriot followed him to London soon afterwards. He set up home and business at Cornhill near the New Exchange. Within a month of his arrival at Court he was one of three men to be appointed Jewellers to the King. For the next five years he amassed another huge fortune and was as much banker as goldsmith.

Heriot's wife died in 1608 and about a year later he returned to Scotland to marry Alison, eldest daughter of James Primrose, Clerk to the Privy Council in Scotland (his grandson became 1st Earl of Rosebery). The couple returned to London and Heriot found himself so busy he was unable to keep up with the demand for his services. He explained the reason for the delays in executing orders to the King who immediately ordered an official notice to all local authorities directing them to assist 'His Majesty's Jeweller in taking up of such workmen as he shall use for the furthering of the service.'

Heriot was heartbroken when his wife died in 1613. He was now fifty years old and such was his grief that he never remarried, preferring to live alone and absorb himself in work. Realising that his vast fortune would be inherited solely by his neice, who lived in Genoa, Italy, he decided to make his intentions known. He made provision for other relatives and executed a disposition and assignation dated 3rd September 1613, leaving the bulk of his wealth for 'the education of children of decayed burgesses and freemen of Edinburgh … ' and to ' … puir orphans and the fatherless children of freemen of the burgh of Edinburgh' with the proviso that they be 'kept at Schule and pious exercises'. And so George Heriot's Hospital (now School) was endowed and completed in 1659 when the first thirty boys took up residence. Building actually started in 1628 but Cromwell used it as a hospital for his troops after the Battle of Dunbar in 1650 until 1659. Additional money from his estates was invested in land, the feus from which paid for the extension (in 1886-88) and maintenance of the Heriot-Watt College (now University).

About the time of his wife's death, Queen Anne owed George Heriot £18,000 and in 1620 he was granted three years imposition on sugar as compensation for his financial assistance to the Royal family. In one of her letters to Heriot, Queen Anne asked him 'to send me two hundrethe pundis vithe all expidition' for a visit to her son in Stirling.

'Jinglin' Geordie' died in 1624 and was buried in London at St Martin's in the Fields. Several 'George Heriot Hospitals' were built in the city, (in one of which the author's grandfather, David Dick, was a prizewinner in 1875) and the land and property which he purchased in his lifetime became part of the Heriot Trust but it is the magnificent Renaissance building modelled on Christ's Hospital, London — George Heriot's School, almost opposite the Royal Infirmary, which is his finest memorial.

6 Howe Street

As you proceed westwards along Heriot Row the first turning to the right is Howe Street, the stepped tenements of which were first feued in 1807. Howe Street commemorates Richard, 1st Earl Howe, a famous British Admiral who prevented two French ships from supplying troops and ammunition to 'Bonnie Prince Charlie' during the '45 Rebellion and served with great distinction in the Seven Years War. He became First Lord of the Admiralty (1783), took command of the Channel Fleet in 1793, gained the 'Glorious 1st of June' off Ushant and brought to an end the mutiny of seamen at the Nore in 1797.

He was born in London on 8th March 1726, one of three brothers who held high rank in the Seven Years War. The other two were Lord George Augustus, the eldest, a Brigadier who was described by General Wolfe as, 'the best officer in the British Army'; he was killed at the British assault on Fort Ticonderoga in 1758 and William, a Colonel who distinguished himself at General Wolfe's victory at Quebec.

After schooling at Eton, Richard entered the navy on 16th July 1739, aged thirteen, on board the Pearl. A year later, he was on his way round the world with Anson's voyage but his ship,' the Severn, was forced to return after a severe storm at Cape Horn. In 1742 he was at the attack on La Guayra in the West Indies and in Antigua he passed his lieutenant's examinations on 24th May 1744. Next day he was appointed full lieutenant and six months later he was given his first command — the sloop Baltimore, and he was posted to the North Sea.

After further action in the Mediterranean, then at the Barbary Coast and later in defence of the Channel Islands he, as captain of the Dunkirk, was ordered to Newfoundland, under Vice-Admiral Sir Edward Boscawen, to waylay the French transport ships carrying 3,000 troop reinforcements. The British and French were in a state of uneasy peace but the French had decided to alter the balance of power in their favour. On 6th June 1755 the French ships were sighted and when challenged they responded, 'Are we at peace or war?' Captain Howe replied, 'At peace' and fired on the Lys and on the Dauphin which promptly surrendered. The

French Captain was heard to remark, 'Behold! a very singular kind of peace, or rather a war declared in a very singular manner!'

Howe was elected MP for Dartmouth in 1756, a seat he held for twenty-six years. But his naval career was by no means ended; in 1758 he commanded the biggest ship in the British Navy, the 74-gun Magnanime, captured from the French, with which he annihilated Aix. However, after the attack on St Malo in 1758, he was disgusted with Marlborough's orgy of destruction of £500,000 worth of shipping and he quickly re-embarked his men when he received news of the approach of the French troops. British losses were heavy and questions relating to the obvious mismanagement were raised in the House of Commons; Howe received praise however for his part in the operation.

On the death of his elder brother, who was killed when the British were defeated at Fort Ticonderoga on 5th July 1758, he succeeded as 4th Viscount Howe of the Irish peerage while serving on the Magnanime in the Bay of Biscay. Shortly afterwards he was appointed Flag-Captain to Prince Edward, Duke of York, in the Princess Amelia.

At the end of the Seven Years War, Howe was a Lord of the Admiralty under Lord Sandwich and Lord Egmont and in August 1765 he was appointed Treasurer of the Navy. He resigned this office on his promotion to Rear-Admiral on 18th October 1770 to take

ST VINCENT STREET AND ST STEPHEN CHURCH

command in the Mediterranean but this appointment was annulled when the dispute with Spain over the Falklands Islands was settled peacefully.

His promotion to Vice-Admiral coincided with that of his brother General Sir William Howe who was in command of the army in North America 'to treat with the revolted Americans, and to take measures for the restoration of peace in the Colonies'. However, war was unavoidable after the American Declaration of Independence on 4th July 1776. The two brothers refused to serve under the Earl of Carlisle on the Commission to negotiate peace and Vice-Admiral Howe, whose promotion had been delayed, realised that he was likely to become a ministerial scapegoat and sought permission to resign his command. In the intervening period he took up a strong position at the Delaware to await reinforcements. The French, under Admiral D'Estaing, with much larger ships, attempted to assist the Americans but could not venture near Howe's ships for fear of running aground. A strong gale dispersed them, Howe's reinforcements arrived and he put to sea to tackle the scattered enemy. Howe was replaced by Rear-Admiral Gambier and on his return home he had to defend his conduct in the House of Commons; he successfully challenged the mismanagement and incompetent ministerial interference.

For the next three years he retired to his country estate near St Albans and attended the House of Commons occasionally. The change of Government in 1782 called him back to active service as Commander-in-Chief in the Channel; he was promoted Admiral of the Blue and created a peer of Great Britain — Viscount Howe of Langar in Nottinghamshire. After a few weeks in the North Sea watching the Dutch off Texel he returned to the Channel to keep it open against forty French and Spanish sail-of-the-line which were allied with America. He relieved Gibraltar against an enormously superior French and Spanish fleet under Cordova who acknowledged that he had been completely outwitted — a victory said to be 'the finest of the war'.

In January 1783 Howe was appointed First Lord of the Admiralty but felt poorly supported by Pitt; he resigned and was created Earl Howe. In May 1790 he was again in command in the Channel as Senior Ad-

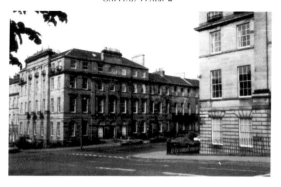

GREAT KING STREET FROM HOWE STREET

miral of the White. The 26 ships of the French fleet
under Admiral Villaret Joyeuse were about equal in
strength to the British fleet. Howe encountered his enemy 300 miles west of Ushant. For four days the two
sides manoeuvered for advantage and on 1st June Howe
broke through the French line to take six prizes and
sink another — this was the 'Glorious 1st of June' hailed
as a magnificent victory. On his return to Spithead on
20th June, George III and Queen Charlotte with three
Princesses were rowed out to visit Howe on board the
Queen Charlotte to present Admiral Howe with a dia-
mond-hilted sword and a promise of the Order of the
Garter.

After his promotion to Admiral of the Fleet in 1796
he presided over the court martial of Vice-Admiral
Cornwallis and he was specially requested by George
III to settle the mutiny at the Nore; this was his last
Naval duty. The genuine grievances of the sailors were
recognised by Howe and the men accepted the assur-
ances of their trusted Admiral, or 'Black Dick' as he
was affectionately known. They returned to sea on 16th
May 1797 to relieve Admiral Duncan at Texel.

Howe had retired from active service just before
the mutiny and lived for only two years more. He died,
aged seventy-six, on 5th August 1799 and was buried
in the family vault at Langar. His monument, by John
Flaxman, in St Paul's Cathedral, London was erected
by public subscription. He was described by Walpole
as 'undaunted as a rock and as silent'.

7   *Gloucester Lane*

At the western end of Heriot Row, Gloucester Lane leads to Gloucester Place which was designed to link Royal Circus across India Street to Doune Terrace and thus into Moray Place. It is part of the Reid and Sibbald scheme of 1822 designed by Thomas Bonnar who was the Heriot Trust Surveyor.

The Gloucester Streets are named after William Frederick, 2nd Duke of Gloucester in keeping with other royal names in the streets of the northern New Town. He was born in 1776 only son of William Henry, 1st Duke of Gloucester at Teodoli Palace in Rome. His mother was the beautiful and witty Maria, dowager countess of Waldegrave, an illegitimate daughter of Sir Edward Walpole — their marriage was kept secret and after its discovery they were banished from Court and lived in Italy until they found royal favour again in 1870. Their son William Frederick resided at Trinity College, Cambridge where he received the degree of MA in 1790. He received the degree of Doctor of Laws, LL.D, in 1796 and was elected a Fellow of the Royal Society (FRS) in 1797.

Prince William's army career started in 1789 with a captain's commission in the 1st Regiment of Foot Guards in which he was given the rank of colonel. He was made full colonel in 1794 and his gallantry earned him the rank of lieutenant-general when he served under Sir David Dundas in 1799 in the Helder expedition.

In 1801 George III made him one of the twenty-five Knights of the Garter and in 1806 he was made a Privy Councillor. In 1808 William, now Duke of Gloucester, was promoted to general, then field marshal in 1816. His father had died in 1805 and he had succeeded to the title as 2nd Duke of Gloucester and Edinburgh and to the Earldom of Connaught. His other titles included GCB — Knight Grand Cross of the Order of the Bath (1815), GCH — Knight Grand Cross of the Royal Guelphic Order (of Hanover, 1815) and Governor of Portsmouth in 1827.

In politics his contribution was not particularly significant but as President of the African Institution he was a strong supporter of the rights of negroes. His sense of justice and fair play led him to support Queen

GLOUCESTER PLACE

Caroline against George IV when the latter tried unsuccessfully to have his Divorce Bill pushed through Parliament in 1820. He supported Catholic Emancipation but opposed Earl Grey's Reform Bill of 1832.

His eighteen years of married life to Mary, fourth daughter of George III, were spent mostly in retirement and in taking an active interest in charities to which he gave most of his income. He died on 30th November 1834.

8 Moray Place

We enter Moray Place via Darnaway Street. Moray Place is one of the most beautiful and prestigious squares in Edinburgh. It was designed as a duodecagonal (twelve-sided) by James Gillespie Graham and built between 1822 and 1855 on

the lands of the Earl of Moray (1531-70) after whom it is named. Continuing round Moray Place to the left we pass Forres Street, which links Moray Place with Queen Street. Darnaway Street and Forres Street take their names from Darnaway Castle near Forres, one of the seats of the Earl of Moray.

Doune Terrace, at the southern end of Moray Place, takes its name from one of the titles of the Earl of Moray — Lord Doune of Doune Castle, near Stirling.

We now enter the two opposing crescents of Ainslie Place which was named after the second wife of the 10th Earl, Lord Moray. She was the second daughter of Sir Philip Ainslie, and was married in 1801; she died in 1837.

Before leaving the Roman Doric pilasters of Ainslie Place we pass St Colme Street which is the continuation of Queen Street and was named after Inchcolme, one of the small islands in the Firth of Forth, of which the Earl of Moray was commendator in the 16th century.

Great Stuart Street links Ainslie Place to Moray Place and it too is named after James Stuart, the 'Good Regent', Earl of Moray and half-brother of Mary Queen of Scots.

James Stuart, Earl of Moray, was the illegitimate son of James V of Scotland by Lady Margaret Erskine. In 1536 he was granted the lands of Tantallon in East Lothian and at age seven he was made Prior (for life) of St Andrews and Mâcon in France. He was educated at St Andrews from 1541 to 1544 and was a pupil of John Knox during 1555 until Knox returned to Geneva.

In 1561 he was sent to France to arrange the return of Mary Queen of Scots, his half-sister. He became her Prime Minister in recognition of which, and after several years of pleading, she created him Earl of Moray and Earl of Mar even though he was a moderate Reformer and she a strict Catholic. At first the arrangement worked; she tried to avoid confrontation with John Knox who tried desperately to convert her to Protestantism while Moray tried to smooth her relationships with the Protestants and with the Queen of England, Elizabeth I.

Lord James Stuart, a calm, modest man could be blunt in speech but he gave nothing away of his personality. His education and bearing made him superior to other Scottish nobles; he was a brilliant leader and showed his genius (and ruthlessness) in quelling the Border bandits (said to have been led by Bothwell) and, with other nobles, he defeated the Earl of Huntly at Corrichie, following Huntly's rebellion in 1562. Moray accompanied Mary during her first tour of the north and he was rewarded with the Huntly estates and possessions. He lived, at that time, fairly close to Queen Mary, at Croft-an-Righ or the King's croft, a sixteenth century picturesque house in the north garden of Holyroodhouse. His marriage in 1562 to Agnes Keith, eldest daughter of William, the Earl Marischal of Scotland, was conducted by John Knox in St Giles Cathedral.

In 1565 Mary married her cousin, the weak and arrogant Henry Stuart, Lord Darnley, the lineal heir to the English throne. Moray refused initially to assent to this marriage and, backed by John Knox and the Hamiltons, he was plainly against it. Because of this Moray fled to England but returned in 1566 the day after the murder of David Rizzio, Mary's Italian secretary. Darnley's jealousy of the talented Rizzio was behind this dastardly murder but Darnley himself was then murdered by Bothwell and about the time of Bothwell's mock trial in which he was acquitted, Moray left for France. Bothwell, full of confidence, carried a not unwilling Mary off to Dunbar. He had divorced his newly wedded wife and was created Duke of Orkney by Mary. They were married only three months after Darnley's murder. The Scottish nobles were up in arms; she was defeated at Carberry and imprisoned at Lochleven where she abdicated in favour of her baby son who was crowned King James VI at Stirling. But Mary escaped and headed her 6000-strong army against the nobles.

The Earl of Moray was recalled and appointed Regent. He marched his forces on 13th May 1568 to Langside and roundly defeated Mary and her army. She fled to England and after being involved in plot after plot she was imprisoned by Elizabeth I who reluctantly signed her death warrant in 1587. Moray, who was appointed Regent in August 1567, was one of the Commissioners who was involved in the case against Mary.

The 'Good Regent' brought peace at last, even managing to settle the troubles of the Church. However, Catholics were hostile to him as were some Protestant Lords — Argyle hated him through their family quarrel and the Hamiltons were jealous of his Regency. An assassination attempt was frustrated in 1568 but two years later James Hamilton of Bothwellhaugh, who harboured a grudge against Moray, shot him in Linlithgow in January 1570.

Moray's death was mourned over all Scotland as its blackest day. Hamilton was banished forever. John Knox shed tears of grief when he conducted his funeral service in St Giles during which 'he moved three thousand persons to tears for the loss of such a good and Godly governor'. He was buried in the south aisle of St Giles and his Coat of Arms is depicted in one of the few surviving brass tablets.

9   *Randolph Crescent*

Randolph Crescent was built in the Moray estate in the 1820s. The entrances to its prestigious houses have round arches and Roman Doric pilasters. Randolph Place, also off Queensferry Street, leads to Randolph Lane, a cul-de-sac at the back of St George's Church, now West Register House. Randolph Cliff with its impressive balconied tenements was designed in 1850 and looks over the valley of the Water of Leith and Thomas Telford's Dean Bridge (built from 1829-31).

The Randolph streets are named after Sir Thomas Randolph who was created Earl of Moray by his uncle, King Robert the Bruce. The line died after the death of his two sons. It was revived in 1562 when Mary Queen of Scots created her half-brother, James Stuart, Earl of Moray, (see number 8 above).

Thomas Randolph was one of Bruce's most loyal supporters from the year 1308. He expelled the English from Edinburgh Castle shortly before the Battle of Bannockburn in 1314 when Bruce routed Edward II's army. His capture of the Castle was one of several daring escapades. With thirty men Randolph scaled the Castle rock in the darkness. An English sentinel surprised them by shouting and throwing a stone over their heads. Imagining that they had been discovered the Scots clung to their ladders and waited. There were no more stones, no more shouts, only silence greeted them. They then crept over the Castle wall and caught the English completely by surprise. Bruce was well pleased, as all the major Scottish strongholds except Stirling Castle had by then been retaken from the English.

Edward II was determined to relieve Stirling Castle by Midsummer's day of 1314, notwithstanding the fact that the English commander of the Castle had agreed to surrender to Bruce by that date to avoid a bloody siege. But the English army arrived, outnumbering the Scots by three to one. Bruce, forever observant, sent Sir Thomas Randolph to prevent nine hundred English cavalry, under Lord Clifford, from reaching Stirling Castle. Sir James Douglas, fearing for his friend's life, went to his aid but soon discovered that Randolph's infantry had the situation well in hand. Douglas turned back to allow Randolph full credit for his victory. Randolph returned to the scene of the battle to command a division; one of four, the others being commanded by Edward, brother of King Robert, Sir James Douglas and Bruce himself whose tactics and bravery won the day to drive the English out of Scotland.

In 1318 Randolph regained Berwick-on-Tweed which was previously lost to Edward I — the 'Hammer of the Scots' as he styled himself when he defeated John Balliol, King of Scots in 1296.

Randolph was created Earl of Moray, a territorial earldom which included Morayshire and its Royal Burghs with wide powers of jurisdiction. He signed the Declaration of Arbroath of 1320 with eight earls, several barons and freeholders who, through it, petitioned the Pope to recognise Scotland's independence and Bruce as their King. Little heed was paid to it by the English and the raids into England continued. Randolph led sorties in 1320 and 1327 with Sir James Douglas (known as 'Black Douglas' by the English) into Northumberland and Durham. Edward simply could not match the guerrilla tactics of the Scots and agreed, in 1328, to a treaty signed in Northampton. The thirty years War of Independence had ended and it appeared that Scotland had won her freedom. Bruce died a year later and Thomas Randolph, Earl of Moray had been chosen by Bruce as Regent until his son David was old enough to reign. Randolph remained Regent until his death in 1332. The peace of 1328, however, did not last long; Edward Balliol, son of John Balliol, invaded Scotland less than a year after David's coronation and

Randolph died suddenly at Musselburgh when he was preparing for battle against Balliol in 1332.

10 Queensferry Street

The 'Queen' of Queensferry is Queen Margaret and Queensferry Road is the main road from the centre of Edinburgh to Queensferry where pilgrims crossed the River Forth to worship at St Andrew's shrine in the 11th century.

Margaret was born about 1045; her father was the English Prince Edward, son of Edmund Ironside. Prince Edward was in exile when he married Agatha, a German Princess, niece of the wife of St Stephen of Hungary. Margaret was brought up by and educated in the Hungarian Court where she learned her strong sense of justice and her saintly ways. She arrived in England, aged eight, to the Court of Edward the Confessor and in 1068 she had to flee to Scotland with her mother and brother, Edgar, with the advent of the Norman Conquest. Her father, after forty years in exile, had been murdered only two days after his arrival in England with his family.

Margaret was the Queen of Malcolm III, Malcolm Canmore. Initially she refused his hand in marriage because her first wish was to become a nun. They met on board ship while anchored in the Firth of Forth when the king came to visit the Saxon fugitives. He was captivated by her beauty and he welcomed the visitors with warmth.

After her marriage to Malcolm III in 1070 they settled in the Palace of Dunfermline which she transformed into a beautiful home and gardens. She transformed Malcolm too; he gave up his manly pursuits and began to spend his evenings in prayer. Her eight children were subjected to strict discipline and she devoted herself to the Church and charity, receiving the guidance and friendship of the Benedictine, Lanfranc, a humble and saintly man who, when he became Archbishop of Canterbury, sent the Chaplain Turgot in his place. Turgot recorded her life, and his written work became the main source of information about her.

It is said that she washed the feet of the poor and gave generously of her resources. Her charitable works however were not merely local; she was painfully aware that, because of the fighting between the Scots and English, hundreds of families fled into the south of Scotland only to become serfs. Queen Margaret sent her envoys to release them and to give them support.

The pilgrims who travelled from afar suffered many privations to pay homage at the eighth-century Church at St Andrew's shrine. Their sufferings on the journey, the cost in crossing 'the sea which divides Lothian from Scotland' and the absence of any form of shelter accounted for much hunger and death. Queen Margaret learned of their plight and made provision for ferrying them across from the embarkation point, which was named Queensferry.

The king, although somewhat uncouth in comparison to his beautiful, serious and saintly wife, was very proud of her; he admired her ability to read and even though he could not read himself he had her books bound and embossed in gold. He supported her charities and her request to meet with clan and religious leaders of the Celtic Church. Her purpose was to try to convince them to give up their fasts and festivals and follow the doctrines of the Communion of Rome. It took her three days of persuasion and argument; her husband translated her eloquent pleas into Gaelic, the Church leaders ultimately agreed and Scotland became a Catholic nation.

For twenty years she pursued her good works; she was blessed and loved by her people but, alas, she was mortal and illness confined her to bed. To make matters worse her husband and her two elder sons had gone south to avenge the insult of William Rufus in his attempts to subordinate Malcolm to become his vassal. Margaret had a premonition of treachery and death and four days later when Prince Edgar approached his mother on her deathbed, she already knew the worst. She died on 16th November 1093.

Malcolm's brother then attacked Edinburgh Castle in an attempt to seize the throne. Queen Margaret's enshrouded body was carried in secret from her Chapel during the darkness of night to be ferried across to Dunfermline to the Church which she and Malcolm had built. Twenty years later Malcolm's body was brought from its burial place in Tynemouth to be laid beside his saintly wife. When Margaret's fourth son became King David I he founded the Abbey at Holyroodhouse and laid his mother's precious black crucifix in the Chapel. She was canonised in 1251 by Innocent IV.

11 *Melville Street and Statue*

Melville Street is 108ft/
33m wide and is the cen-
tral avenue of the Walker
development. The three
spires of St Mary's Ca-
thedral are straight
ahead — this is the West-
ern New Town. The ar-
chitect was Robert
Brown; the land had
been purchased by
William Walker for his
son Sir Patrick Walker
and Brown added to the
original plan of James
Gillespie Graham, the
streets of Manor Place,
Walker Street and
Coates Crescent in 1814.

Melville Crescent,
half way along Melville
Street is, in fact, a square
set diagonally with the
statue of Robert Dundas,
2nd Viscount Melville
(1771-1851), by John Steell in 1857 in its centre. He
was the son of Henry Dundas, 1st Viscount Melville
(1742-1811) after whom Melville Street is named and
whose biography appears in Capital Walk 1, number
25 on page 86.

Robert Saunders Dundas, 2nd Viscount Melville,
was the only son of the all-powerful Henry Dundas, 1st
Viscount Melville. Although Robert would become a
Privy Councillor and President of the Board of Trade,
he would never reach the fame or exert the power and
influence of his father. In fact, the Dundas dynasty qui-
etly ended with the son.

He was educated at the High School of Edinburgh
and as MP for Hastings he entered Parliament in 1794,
aged just twenty-one. Immediately he became Private
Parliamentary Secretary to his father who was Secretary of State for War and the Colonies as well as President of the Board of Control for the affairs of India.

Young Robert saw overt power in action. His father, a close friend of Prime Minister William Pitt, had almost complete control of the Scottish members and therefore of Scottish affairs. That his son should become Solicitor-General and Lord Advocate of Scotland was hardly surprising. Lord Cockburn in his *Memorials* describes him:

> Dundas had two qualifications which made him not merely the best Lord Advocate that his party could have supplied, but really a most excellent one … He was a little, alert, handsome, gentleman-like man, with a countenance and air beaming with sprightliness and gaiety, and dignified by considerable fire; altogether inexpressibly pleasing. It was impossible not to like the owner of that look.

In 1796 Robert Dundas married Anne Saunders and added her name to his own. She was an heiress and great-niece of Admiral Charles Saunders, famed for running the gauntlet with great skill and daring, up the St Lawrence River against the French at Quebec in July 1759. In the year of his marriage Robert Dundas was elected MP for Rye and in 1800 he was appointed one of the Keepers of the Signet for Scotland. In 1801 he was elected MP for Midlothian and when his father came under attack in the House of Commons he spoke with great spirit in his defence. In 1805, when Henry Dundas was openly accused and impeached for misusing his office as Treasurer of the Navy, Robert spoke heatedly in his father's favour. It was clear that he had inherited much of the Dundas eloquence.

He was made a Privy Councillor in March 1807 and in April he was given a seat in the Cabinet as President of the Board of Control in the ministry of the Duke of Portland. He had been given this appointment in consideration of his father's great powers of administration and service to the Tory party. In 1809 he was made Irish Secretary but after six months he returned to his previous post of President of the Board of Control under the Percival administration.

His father died in 1811 and he became 2nd Viscount Melville. He was appointed First Lord of the

Admiralty in 1812 and in this office he gave competent service as a talented administrator for the next fifteen years. He took a keen interest in and gave support and encouragement to the Arctic expeditions which was recognised in the naming of Viscount Melville Sound in northern Canada in his honour.

In addition to several appointments in Scotland he was Lord Privy Seal, a Governor of the Bank of Scotland and Chancellor of the University of St Andrews. He was made one of the sixteen Knights of The Most Ancient and the Most Noble Order of the Thistle (KT) in 1821.

The growing pressure for electoral reform and for Roman Catholic Emancipation was too much for Robert Dundas. He refused office in the Canning administration and resigned office in 1827. However, he accepted reappointment at the Admiralty under the Duke of Wellington's administration in 1828, but Wellington buckled under the pressure for reform and the passing of Roman Catholic Emancipation in 1829 finally forced Dundas's resignation. So ended the great Dundas family's rule in Scotland. He retired from political life in 1830 and settled at Melville Castle where he died on 10th June 1851 at the age of eighty.

12 Walker Street

Walker Street was built in two parts north and south of Melville Crescent — the south section first in 1822-27 and the north section in 1827-45. Coates Crescent, opposite Atholl Crescent, was the first to be built in the Western New Town, starting in 1813. It is split by Walker Street.

These streets are named after the owner of the estates of Coates and Drumsheugh, Sir Patrick Walker. He was the second son of William Walker, Attorney in Exchequer and proprietor of the estates of Coates in the West End, after whom William Street was named. Patrick Walker was born in 1777 and he qualified as an advocate on 17th April 1798 but he did not feel the need to practice law as he had just inherited a large fortune. With the threat of invasion in 1797, (France having declared war against Britain and Holland on 31st January 1793), Patrick Walker joined the Horse and Artillery Corps and afterwards the Militia in which he held the rank of lieutenant-colonel.

In 1805 his father paid £7,000 so that his son Patrick would hold the office of Heritable Usher of the White Rod of Scotland. Patrick Walker took the duties of the office very seriously and he petitioned King George III and the government with several claims over a period of several years. In many instances he exceeded the requirements of the office, for example as a County Magistrate, a Commissioner of Improvements, a Road Trustee and in many other capacities. He was concerned with most of the charitable institutions of the City of Edinburgh and for his conscientious services and the great respect in which he was held he was given a knighthood. He was also active in many literary and scientific societies; his special interest in the Society of Antiquaries, the Society of Arts and the Wernerian Natural History Society earned him a reputation of considerable distinction; in his day he had few equals in the fields of antiquaries and natural history.

At the state entry to Edinburgh of George IV in 1822 (lavishly organised by Sir Walter Scott), Sir Patrick Walker 'was the most splendid beyond comparison of any that graced the ceremony'. He rode his white charger resplendent in gold and scarlet and after his death he was described 'as a bright example of a patriotic and public-spirited citizen'. In 1829 Sir Patrick organised the procession for the opening of the new High School on the southern side of the Calton Hill. It was 'preceded by the band of the 17th Lancers, each class marching with a master at its head, followed by the High Constables, the magistrates, professors of the university and all "those noblemen and gentlemen who had attended the High School in fours".'

Sir Patrick Walker died on 3rd October 1837, four months after the death of William IV and the accession of Queen Victoria. The estates of Coates and Drumsheugh with the office of the Heritable Usher of the White Rod passed to Sir Patrick's two sisters, Mary and Barbara Walker. When Mary died in 1871, her sister having pre-deceased her, and having had no families, they left 'both lands and office to a permanent body of trustees for the benefit of the Scottish Episcopalian Church and for the creation and endowment of the handsome Cathedral Church of St Mary's, so named from respect to the memory of the mother of Sir Patrick and his sisters'. Their estates, bequeathed in 1870, were considerable and included 'the sites of Coates Crescent, Melville, Walker, Stafford Streets, and other thoroughfares, yielding a rental of about £20,000 yearly and representing a capital of £400,000'.

13 Rothesay Place

Rothesay Place was designed in 1872 (by Peddie and Kinnear) during the reign of Queen Victoria. The eldest son of the monarch is given the titles Prince of Wales, Duke of Rothesay and Duke of Cornwall and in this case refers to Edward VII.

Edward VII, the only monarch of the House of Saxe-Coburg, was born on 9th November 1841 at St James Palace. Queen Victoria and Prince Albert were completely baffled by the behaviour of their eldest son, Prince Albert Edward, or as he was to become affectionately known, 'Bertie'. He was a placid enough baby but in childhood he displayed uncontrolled bouts of temper accompanied by loud and outrageous screaming. His tutors soon became exasperated and, one after the other, gave up their Royal charge as impossible. His younger brothers and sisters suffered his cruel outbursts to such an extent that Baron Stockmar advised that he should not be left without adult supervision in the nursery. Queen Victoria and Albert tried every possible diversion to catch his interest but he made little progress and displayed angry aversion to any scholarship. An attempt, on one occasion, to do some arithmetic resulted in violence — his pencil was tossed away, his stool kicked aside and he cursed his tutor. Latin caused a furore. Prince Albert took over but made lit-

133

tle progress; at least Bertie could not run about and spit at his father.

Aged eighteen he was sent to the University of Edinburgh where, surprisingly, Scottish academics found some talent. Then followed Oxford and Cambridge where he quickly discovered that very little work seemed to satisfy the authorities and he enjoyed himself enormously. The dons hung on his every word and invited him to dine, no doubt enjoying the honour. His fellow students thought differently — they avoided him at every turn.

His visit to Canada and the USA in 1860 was very successful, especially with the young ladies. His father died shortly after an incident which had greatly angered him and which the Queen considered to have shortened Prince Albert's life. It occurred during military manoeuvres in Ireland; the Prince's brother officers, knowing of his fondness for the ladies, smuggled an actress into the Prince's tent during the night. The joke seriously backfired but the Prince resolutely refused to name the officers involved.

In 1863 the Prince of Wales married the beautiful Princess Alexandra of Denmark and, whilst she was welcomed into the British Royal family, the Queen was annoyed when, in 1864, he supported the Danes in their war against Prussia and Austria over Schleswig-Holstein. She was even more annoyed when the Prince supported Prime Minister Lord Palmerston and Lord Russell, the Foreign Secretary, against the German States and when the Prince agreed to meet the Italian revolutionary Giuseppe Garibaldi, who also supported Denmark, she was exasperated to the point of despair.

She even refused to allow the Prince access to State papers and confined his activities to the opening of bridges and public buildings — in fact this started the practice of Royalty accepting engagements to lay foundation stones and perform public ceremonies of this kind. However, the Prince's favourite pastimes were quite different and included eating (five huge meals each day), hunting, shooting, gambling and beautiful women. His friends had to be very rich to afford his company and they included not only the aristocracy, but also rich businessmen, politicians and trade unionists. He became involved in several scandals but managed to have them covered up excepting two court cases in which he was subpoenaed. His involvement with Sir Charles Mordaunt's wife and his participation in an illegal game of baccarat could not be hidden when, in the latter case, Sir William Gordon-Cumming, accused of cheating, sued the players for slander.

Eventually he succeeded Queen Victoria in 1901 aged fifty-nine. His nine-year reign coincided with an era of political progression and the 1906 General Election gave the Liberals an eighty-strong majority under Sir Henry Campbell-Bannerman. His government gave South Africa the right to govern itself, the trade unions the right to peacefully picket and forbade the Courts from taking civil action against them. The social changes included the introduction of the old age pension, National Insurance and the embryo of the modern welfare state but Edward VII supported the Conservatives and was against votes for women. His tours of European countries, especially France, gave him the epithet 'Edward the Peacemaker' but his nephew, the Kaiser William II of Germany, viewed his activities with suspicion. The French Foreign Minister, Declassé, was well pleased when Edward became King; Queen Victoria had favoured Germany and now, the two men were anxious to achieve friendship between the two countries and in 1904 the 'entente cordiale' was reached. The Socialists and some Liberals at home were openly critical of the King's meeting with Czar Nicholas II whose regime of oppression in Russia was deprecated in Britain.

In 1909, when Lloyd George was Chancellor of the Exchequer, the House of Lords turned down his 'War budget' — the war against poverty. This was a constitutional catastrophe not equalled since the Reform Bill of 1832. Edward VII refused Prime Minister Asquith sufficient additional Peers to give him a majority in the Lords, preferring instead to try to negotiate. In the end he insisted on a General Election and in the midst of the crisis he died — on 6th May 1910, aged sixty-eight.

14 Palmerston Place

Leaving Rothesay Place we enter Palmerston Place at its northern end. Its two churches — Palmerston Place Church with its twin domes and the early Gothic St Mary's Episcopal Cathedral with the long established Music School add to the attraction of this street which is named after Henry John Temple Palmerston, 3rd Viscount.

Lord Palmerston, Foreign Secretary in 1830 and 1846, Prime Minister in 1855, 1857 and 1859, supporter of the Reform Bill of 1832 and heartily disliked by Queen Victoria was more of a modern day president than a Prime Minister. He was tough debater whose interfering ways in foreign affairs gave him the reputation of 'Firebrand Palmerston'.

Palmerston was born on 20th October 1784 at Broadlands in Hampshire. He was educated at Harrow, then at Edinburgh University in 1800, where he boarded with the Professor of Moral Philosophy, Dugald Stewart, the disciple of Reid's commonsense philosophy.

At St John's College, Cambridge, he found his studies fairly simple after Edinburgh. He obtained his MA degree without examination (this was a privilege of noblemen at that time; Palmerston had succeeded his father in 1802). In his last year as a student he stood for the Parliamentary seat of his University (vacant because of the death of William Pitt in 1806) but failed to be elected. However, the following year he was successful in Newton, Isle of Wight and in 1811 he gained the seat of his University and held it until 1831 when his support for the Reform Bill lost him this seat — he had disassociated himself from the Tories in 1828.

When the Duke of Wellington resigned in 1830 over the Reform Bill, Earl Grey became Prime Minister and he offered Palmerston the Foreign Office. For the first time Britain and France became allies. It was largely due to Palmerston that Belgium gained its independence from Holland . He successfully brought about the quadruple alliance (1834) between Britain, France, Portugal and Spain and he was largely instrumental in the enthronement of Isabella of Spain and Maria of Portugal. He thwarted Russia's ambitions by saving Turkey at the expense of unpopularity with Egypt.

Palmerston used tough language and displayed little sympathy for other nations but he worked tirelessly to get rid of slave trading and publicly praised the London Barclay and Perkins draymen for manhandling the Austrian General, Baron Haynau, (the ruthless flogger of women, nicknamed the 'hyena of Brescia') after the draymen had rolled him in the mud.

When the Whigs resigned over free trade in 1841, Palmerston was replaced by the high-minded Lord Aberdeen but he was back again in 1846 as Foreign Secretary under Lord John Russell.

Palmerston's second term in the Foreign Office was made difficult and embarrassing when Francois Guizot, the French King's chief adviser checkmated Palmerston over the 'Spanish Marriages' in which French royalty gained influence in Spain finding husbands for the young Queen Isabella and her sister. Palmerston and Queen Victoria were furious; the 'entente cordiale' disintegrated.

In 1848 Europe was again in the midst of revolution; the French radicals overthrew the Orleanist throne, the revolts in Hungary and Vienna brought down the Metternich system, the Prussian monarchy was threatened by the Weimar government, the Italian revolt against the Austrians was led by Savoy but Czardom survived. Palmerston however made enemies, his haughty, autocratic methods in the foreign office and abroad provoked fury; the Sicilian rebels received arms from Woolwich arsenal at Palmerston's direction and in 1850 his over-reaction in sending a naval squadron to threaten the Greek government into paying a debt due to a Gibraltar Jew, Don Pacifico, who claimed to be a British subject — all led to a vote of censure by the House of Lords. He survived the vote of the Commons. However, the following year he pre-empted approval of Napoleon's coup d'état without consulting either the Prime Minister or the Queen and was dismissed.

In 1852 Palmerston was appointed Home Secretary in Lord Aberdeen's coalition and in 1853 he advocated sending the British fleet into the Black Sea to defend Turkey against Russian aggression but his advice was unheeded and war broke out in 1854. The British army had been woefully neglected and the horrors of this war destroyed Aberdeen's government in 1855. Palmerston became Prime Minister and immediately set about retrieving the British failure — he went to war with vigour; Britain, France and Austria drew up the agreement — part of Bessarabia to go to Rumania, international control of the Danube for navigation, rejection of Russia's naval power in the Black Sea. However, the old Czar would hear none of it and the war continued. In 1855 the new Czar, Alexander II, finally accepted the agreement and peace was signed in March 1856. The cost to Britain was 25,000 men and £50 million.

On Richard Cobden's successful motion against the Chinese war in 1857 in which Palmerston was defeated by sixteen votes, he called an election and was returned handsomely (Cobden lost his seat). Within a year, however, Palmerston's government fell over his defeat over the Conspiracy Bill; a bomb had been thrown at Napoleon III by an Italian, Orsini, who had hatched the plot and made the weapons in England. Disraeli became Prime Minister but he too lost power over his attempt at parliamentary reform — the 'fancy franchises' as Bright described it.

Palmerston was Premier again in 1859, (not the choice of Queen Victoria who preferred the courtly Granville). The Liberal Party consisted of the Canningites, the Whigs, the Peelites and the Radicals. Palmerston was popular; he had increased national prosperity but foreign policy was his strong suit. He continued to disagree at Court but agreement was reached on the need for national defence. In 1862 the Americans were in the midst of their Civil War and in 1864 Bismark declared war by pulling the Austrians with him against the Danes. Palmerston, encouraging the Danes, was vehemently opposed by the Queen and his cabinet; he was dubbed 'extremely impertinent' by Her Majesty. Parliament was dissolved and Palmerston, now eighty, was re-elected with a comfortable majority but he had to find another constituency in Lancashire — Oxford University having sacked him (as they had his leader Peel in 1829) because of his famous declaration 'that every man was morally entitled to a vote who was not positively incapacited by unfitness'.

Palmerston died two days before his eighty-first birthday and was buried in Westminster Abbey.

15 Glencairn Crescent

The first pair of crescents off Palmerston Place, Glencairn Crescent and Eglinton Crescent, were said to have been named by their builder, James Steel, to remind us of an ancient rivalry between the two noble families. The designer was John Chesser and Glencairn Crescent was built between 1873 and 1879.

The 1st Earl of Glencairn, Alexander Cunningham, was created by James III in May 1488; two weeks later he was killed at the Battle of Sauchieburn on 11th June 1488 during which James III was thrown from his horse and murdered by rebels said to have been led by his son.

The Earls of Glencairn were descended from Cunningham of Kilmaurs in Ayrshire (hence the name of Kilmaurs Road in the Grange district). The first Earl, Alexander Cunningham, was created a Lord of Parliament with the title Lord Kilmaurs in 1463. Some notable Earls of Glencairn were the 3rd, William Cunningham, who was taken prisoner after the Battle of Solway Moss. In 1557 the 4th Earl of Glencairn, as one of the 'Lords of the Congregation', drew up the First Covenant which was the first step against the Queen Regent, Mary of Guise, towards Protestantism. He was an ardent supporter of John Knox and was party to the murder of Rizzio, Mary Queen of Scots' secretary. After Mary was deposed Kirkcaldy of Grange with Maitland of Lethington planned to restore her to the throne by the capture of the King's Lords — Argyle, Glencairn, Sutherland, Cassillis, Eglinton and Regent Lennox. All but Lennox escaped.

During the Civil War (1642-46) the 9th Earl of Glencairn was appointed one of Charles II's Commissioners; Glencairn, as Chancellor and General Middleton, also a Commissioner, headed a rising in 1654 but it was severely crushed by General Monck at Dalnaspidal.

The 14th Earl of Glencairn (1749-91), James Cunningham befriended Robert Burns, Scotland's national bard, and introduced him to his tutor, William Creech, the publisher. Such was Burns's gratitude he composed Verses to be written below a Noble Earl's Picture and such was the Earl's modesty he withheld his consent. Glencairn used his influence to obtain the post of exciseman for Burns who described his 'weight of obligation' to Glencairn as a 'pleasing load'.

The 14th Earl succeeded to the Earldom in 1775 on the death of his father, his elder brother having died in 1768. He was a Captain of the West Fencible Regiment and he was chosen as a Scottish representative peer in 1780. He sold the family estate of Kilmaurs in 1786. In 1790 his health deteriorated and he was advised to spend the winter in Lisbon but as no improvement took place he decided to return home on 30th January 1791. He got no further than Falmouth where he died aged only forty-two. Robert Burns, greatly saddened, wrote the poignant lines:

> *The Bridegroom may forget the Bride*
> *Was made his wedded wife Yestreen;*
> *The Monarch may forget the Crown*
> *That on his head an hour has been;*
> *The Mother may forget the Child*
> *That smiles so sweetly on her knee;*
> *But I'll remember thee Glencairn,*
> *And all that thou hast done for me!*
> *For all I have and all I am I owe to thee!*

The Countess of Glencairn, widow of the 13th Earl, feued the land of West Coates in 1792 where she died in 1801; it was no doubt this which led to the naming of this crescent.

16 Eglinton Crescent

Eglinton Crescent, oppo-
site Glencairn Crescent,
was built between 1875
and 1880 and designed by
John Chesser. It is named
after   Hugh
Montgomerie, the 12th
Earl of Eglinton who en-
joyed the full life of a feudal baron. His thoughts

were as big as his actions — he loved magnificence and
grandeur and he matched his tastes with enterprising
public-spiritedness.

The castle of Eglinton is one of his finest pieces of
modern castellated architecture and his harbour at
Ardrossan was originally meant to be the port of Glasgow; he built it in 1806 but the cost of canal building
proved to be prohibitively expensive. He was an aristocrat of culture; an accomplished musician, he per-
formed the violincello and composed a few popular
airs such as Lady Montgomerie's Lament and Ayrshire
Lassies.

He was born in 1739 the son of Alexander
Montgomerie of Coilsfield in Ayrshire. He entered the
army in 1756 and served in the American War of Independence as a captain in the 78th foot and then in the
1st Royals. He was elected Member of Parliament for
Ayrshire in 1780 and in 1784. He may have shown courage in battle but his speeches in Parliament were poor
— Robert Burns was prompted to write 'I ken, if that
your sword were wanted, Ye'd lend a hand; But when
there's ought to say anent it, Ye're at a stand!'

He returned to army service in 1788 as a major in
the Western Fencibles in the French War. He was re-
elected for Ayrshire again in 1796 but he gave up his
seat on the death of his father and his succession to the
Earldom in June of that year. He inherited 'the noble
domain of Eglinton Castle' south of Kilwinning in Ayrshire and he proceeded to rebuild the elegant mansion
in modern castellated style — this was the seat of the
Montgomeries, the Earls of Eglinton for nearly five
centuries. In addition he now owned the Abbey of
Kilwinning which had been lost by the Earl of Glencairn

in 1603. (This is possibly the rivalry between Eglinton and Glencairn which was referred to by the builder of the two crescents, James Steel, when he named them).

He was elected a representative peer of Scotland in 1798 and again in 1802. George III created him a peer of the United Kingdom in 1806 — Baron Ardrossan of Ardrossan. He was awarded the special honour restricted to sixteen Scotsmen — Knight of The Most Ancient and the Most Noble Order of the Thistle (KT). He was appointed Lord Lieutenant of Ayrshire and a State Councillor to the Prince Regent. He died aged eighty on 15th December 1819.

17 Grosvenor Crescent

Along Palmerston Place and opposite St Mary's Cathedral, is Grosvenor Crescent designed by John Chesser in 1869-71, and the equal and opposite crescent to Lansdowne Crescent. Its three-storey stone houses have magnificent Ionic pilastered doorways with columned porches in its centre.

St Mary's Cathedral owes its existence to two sisters who were heiresses of Sir Patrick Walker (after whom Walker Street is named). The sisters left their fortune for the creation of an Episcopal church to

ST MARY'S EPISCOPAL CATHEDRAL WITH ST MARY'S MUSIC SCHOOL, BELOW

be built on the Palmerston Place site. The result was G. Gilbert Scott's 1872 design of this early Gothic representation, although the two west spires were added by his sons John and Charles Scott in 1913-17. It was designed to seat 1,500 people and cost £110,000 (the original estimate was £45,000) and was built between 1874 and 1917.

Grosvenor Crescent commemorates the Earls of Grosvenor; the 1st Earl was Richard Grosvenor (1731-

1802), eldest son of Sir Robert, 6th Baronet and grandson of Sir Thomas Grosvenor.

The Grosvenor family arrived in England with William the Conqueror in 1066 and settled at Eaton near Chester. Their baronetcy dates from 1622, the Earldom from 1784, the Marquessate from 1831 and the Dukedom of Westminster from 1874. Richard Grosvenor was born on 18th June 1731; he was educated at Oriel College, Oxford where he was 'created' MA in 1751. His father died when Richard was twenty-four and he succeeded as the 7th Baronet having been elected MP for Chester the previous year. In 1758 he added to the family estate of Eaton with the purchase of the manor of Eccleston and the hamlet of Belgrave (Belgravia in London). He was elected Mayor of Chester in 1759 and was grand cupbearer at the Coronation of George III. Prime Minister William Pitt the Elder recommended Richard Grosvenor's elevation as Baron Grosvenor of Eaton in 1761.

His marriage to Henrietta, daughter of Henry Vernon of Hilton Park was happy at first; they had four sons but only their third son, Robert, survived. The marriage became progressively miserable for the baron. Henrietta was vain and took pleasure from the indiscreet attentions of the Duke of Cumberland, brother of George III. He sued the Duke and was awarded damages of £10,000. His great interest was in horse racing and he was a well-known breeder of horses. He died in 1802 at Earl's Court and was succeeded by his son Robert.

Robert Grosvenor, 2nd Earl of Grosvenor, 1st Marquis of Westminster, was born in London on 22nd March 1767 and educated at Harrow and Trinity College, Cambridge where he took his MA degree in 1786. He travelled on the continent with his tutor, William Gifford, and on his return in 1788, he was elected MP for East Looe and appointed Lord of the Admiralty in 1789. Following in his father's footsteps, he was elected MP for Chester in the General Election of 1790. On 28th April 1794 he married Eleanor, daughter of the Earl of Wilton and he inherited the Egerton estates with the Earldom and Viscountcy of Wilton; they had three sons and one daughter. Grosvenor was appointed a Commissioner of the Board of Control between 1793 and 1801 and he represented the City of London until his death in 1802.

The 3rd Earl, 2nd Marquess of Westminster, raised a Volunteer Regiment in which he was Major Commandant during the Revolutionary War. Having succeeded his father in 1802 he started the rebuilding of Eaton Hall a year later. In 1819 he married Lady Elizabeth Leveson-Gower whose parents, the Duke and Duchess of Sutherland, were reputed to be the richest family in Europe. In London, the Earl obtained special powers in 1826 to lay out the roads and streets of the area now known as Belgravia. The land was drained by Thomas Cubitt and the surface clay was used to make the bricks for the prestigious houses. At the Coronation of William IV he was created Marquis of Westminster and the Arms of the City of Westminster were granted to him in 1831; ten years later he was awarded the Order of the Garter.

He died on 17th February 1845 at his favourite residence, Eaton Hall. He was an aristocrat of taste whose contribution to public affairs was considerable. He was a Whig who gave his support to William Pitt and his improvements to Chester included the erection of the North Gate. He was well-known and respected as a successful owner of race-horses.

His son, Hugh Lupus Grosvenor, was born in 1825 and was created a Duke by Queen Victoria in 1874. It was said that she felt that a Dukedom was appropriate because he was even richer than herself. Hugh Lupus's boyhood was somewhat unhappy due to his father's incessant criticism and he, in turn, seemed to have inherited this trait; he considered his sons to be unworthy of the title they would inherit. He was educated at Eton and Balliol College, Oxford and was elected MP for Chester aged twenty-two, a seat he held for twenty-one years. In 1852 he married his cousin Constance who was the fourth daughter of the Duke of Sutherland. He succeeded his father in 1869 and owned 30,000 acres in Cheshire and 600 acres in London. His passion was racehorses and he owned four Derby winners. His wife died in 1880; his second marriage to Catherine Cavendish lasted until his death in 1899; she died in 1941.

The present Duke of Westminster is the richest landowner in the UK, second only to Her Majesty, Queen Elizabeth.

18 Lansdowne Crescent

The late Georgian design of Lansdowne Crescent was executed by Robert Matheson in 1865 with its Italianate cornices and balustraded parapets. It is opposite Grosvenor Crescent and is named after Henry Charles Keith Petty-Fitzmaurice, the 5th Marquis of Lansdowne born in 1845.

After Eton and Balliol he enjoyed the outdoor life of a young aristocrat — hunting, shooting, fishing — before following the family's Liberal traditions in politics. Initially between 1868 and 1883, he was given minor posts in two of Gladstone's administrations; junior Lord of the Treasury in 1869, Under-Secretary for War from 1872 to 1874 and Under-Secretary of State for India in 1880 which he resigned over Gladstone's Irish Home Rule policy; the Irish Land League having withheld the rents of his Irish properties. In 1883 he was appointed Governor-General of Canada and in 1888 Viceroy of India. He returned home in 1895 to become Secretary of State for War and Foreign Secretary in two consecutive Unionist administrations and from 1906 he was leader of the opposition in the House of Lords.

The 5th Marquis of Lansdowne was born on 14th January 1845 at Lansdowne House, Berkeley Square in London. Some of his forebears include: Sir William Petty (1623-87) the economist who was knighted by Charles II; William Petty, 2nd Earl of Shelburne (great-grandson of Sir William) who was Prime Minister in 1782 and who was made 1st Marquis of Lansdowne; the 3rd Marquis who declined the Premiership twice but served as Chancellor of the Exchequer and supported the Reform Bill of 1832.

On the death of his father, Henry Thomas, 4th Marquis, in 1866, he became the 5th Marquis and in 1869 he married Lady Maud Evelyn Hamilton, the youngest of the seven beautiful daughters of the 1st Duke of Abercorn. They had three prestigious houses: Lansdowne in London, Bowood (Adam designed) in Wiltshire and Dereen in Co Kerry in Ireland with its magnificent gardens (destroyed in 1922).

In his five years as Governor-General of Canada (1883-88) he supported the construction of the Canadian-Pacific Railway and was sufficiently popular to survive a personal attack from the Irish Nationalist William O'Brien. On his return to Ireland in 1888 he received an address of welcome from his tenants at Dereen in spite of the troubles. Six months later he left for India to take up the Viceroyship — another successful administration during which he competently handled the Indian currency problem.

After his return home he was appointed Secretary of War (1895-1900) and supported Lord Wolseley as Commander-in-Chief of the British Army. Lansdowne was blamed for the early disasters of the Boer War but the cabinet had failed to take Wolseley's advice and refused to send badly needed reinforcements to South Africa. In 1900 he became Foreign Secretary, a job for which he was ideally suited. He negotiated two important agreements: one with Japan in 1902 and the other with France in April 1904 in which he conceded Newfoundland and Siam but gained in Africa. However, an alliance with Germany proved to be impossible but he made the 'entente-cordiale' with France (1904). Russia was defeated by Japan over Manchuria and Germany, becoming more of a threat, was building her navy.

The Liberals came to power in 1905 and Lansdowne was Conservative leader of the opposition when, in 1909, the House of Lords turned down Lloyd George's 'War Budget' — war against poverty — this was as great a constitutional crisis as the 1832 Reform Bill. Edward VII refused Asquith additional peers and, in the middle of the chaos, he died in May 1910. There had been several other contests between the upper and lower houses and Lansdowne introduced a Bill for the internal reform of the House of Lords. Two general elections produced no change and then Asquith played his master stroke — George V would agree to additional peers. Lansdowne convened a hurried meeting of the Unionist peers; they were split and Lansdowne favoured abstention. His Bill was dropped, the Government having introduced its own Parliamentary Bill.

Twenty years of posturing aggression left Germany without friends, except Austria. On 28th June 1914 Franz-Ferdinand, Archduke of Austria and his wife were assassinated and the Kaiser's support of the Austrian ultimatum led to war. On 2nd August the Germans invaded Luxembourg and demanded passage through

Belgium. On 4th August the Germans were in Belgium and ignored the British ultimatum for Belgian neutrality — the Great War had begun. Lansdowne's meeting with Bonar Law and several other Unionists at Lansdowne House strongly influenced the Cabinet to go to war; the Unionist party had pledged its support for France.

Lansdowne was a member (without portfolio) of Asquith's unwieldy coalition Cabinet until 1916 when it disintegrated over Lansdowne's memorandum in which he proposed a peace accommodation. It was published a year later (in November 1917) and was disowned by the Government and the press. Lansdowne was accused of disloyalty to the cause of the allies and he was ostracised by the Conservatives. He retired from politics but suffered ill health and was deeply affected when his beloved estate Dereen was completely destroyed by the Irish 'Irregulars' in 1922. He died in 1927.

19 Atholl Crescent

Atholl Crescent, designed by Thomas Bonnar in 1825, is named after the Duke of Atholl whose ancestral home is Blair Castle in Blair Atholl. The present 10th Duke, George Iain Murray DL, MA who inherited the title in 1956, is a representative peer of Scotland, chairman of Westminster Press Ltd., and Chairman of the Royal National Lifeboat Institution. He was born on 19th June 1931 and educated at Eton and Christ Church, Oxford. His interests include Scottish wildlife, land ownership (130,000 acres) and the Red Deer Commission. His 80-strong private army is the only one allowed in Britain.

Atholl was one of eleven earldoms of ancient origin. The titles of these earldoms relate to historic regions of Scotland and the earldom of Atholl, previously held by the Strathbogie family, was acquired by the Stewarts on the accession of James I in 1406.

When James I was released from captivity in England his first task was to eliminate his rivals for the crown; it seems that the Earl of Atholl helped to influence him against his chief rival — the powerful Duke of Albany. Albany had served his own interests as Governor of Scotland during James's imprisonment. With Albany removed, Walter, the Earl of Atholl, as the youngest son of Robert II (r.1371-90) was given the earldom of Strathearn which tacitly recognised his place in the royal succession. However, after James I's assassination in 1437 his murderers were caught and brutally tortured to death; Atholl was said to have been put to death by means of a crown of red-hot iron placed upon his head. His grandson was killed with him, thus ending the male line of Robert II's second marriage to Euphemia Ross.

The 1st Duke of Atholl, created in 1703, was John Murray (1659-1724), 2nd Marquis, who was a strong opponent of the government's 'sale' of Scotland which he considered was brought about by bribery to effect the Union of Parliaments in 1707; Atholl himself received £1,000 but this did not change his disdain and dislike of it. At a meeting of the Scottish Parliament he proposed that the Commissioners for the Union should not be authorised until the Alien Act of 1705 (in which Scotsmen were treated as aliens) had been repealed.

He died in 1724 and James (1690-1764), his third son succeeded as 2nd Duke; his first and second sons having pre-deceased him. James's two brothers, Charles and George, supported the 1715 and 1745 Jacobite Risings. George was one of Prince Charles's most clever lieutenant-generals and in 1745 the Atholl men formed a brigade with the Robertsons but many of the latter deserted after their easy victory over Sir John Cope at Prestonpans. Lord John Murray, the Duke's brother, urged the Marquis of Tullibardine, the 2nd Duke's son, to make an example of the deserters by burning their homes and crops.

James, the 2nd Duke, laid claim to the Barony of Strange in England through the Earl of Derby line. His son and one daughter died in childhood and his surviving daughter, Charlotte, married her cousin, John, eldest son of Lord George and John (1729-74) succeeded as the 3rd Duke. In 1727 he received a gift of some larch trees and introduced them for the first time to Scotland. He planted them on the hillsides near Dunkeld. His son, John (1755-1831) the 4th Duke, followed his example by planting twenty-seven million of them and earned the nickname, 'Planting John'. He raised the Atholl Highlanders in 1777 and was a representative peer from 1780 to 1786. He died on the 29th September 1831 and was buried at Dunkeld.

20 *Gladstone Memorial*

When Gladstone's memorial was first placed in the garden of Coates Crescent there were so many objections from residents that it was decided to relocate it at Saint Andrew Square. However, by the mid-1950s it was a traffic hazard and was re-installed in its original 1902 position. In his Chancellor's robes, this magnificent monument, by J. Pittendrigh MacGillivray, is surrounded by eight bronze figures representing his virtues.

William Ewart Gladstone was born in Liverpool in 1809. His father, Sir John Gladstone, after whom Gladstone Place, overlooking Leith Links, is named, was a successful corn merchant in Leith. William was educated at Eton and Oxford where he took a double first degree. He stood for Parliament in 1833 and won his seat at Newark. As a devout Christian his original intention had been to enter the Church but instead he took his religious beliefs into political life. His workload was formidable and from his entry into Parliament, aged twenty-four, his opponents soon discovered his awesome ability as an outstanding debater; with sharp intelligence and alacrity he could identify the minutest weakness in argument and cut through it with the neatness of a surgeon's scalpel.

Within a year of his arrival in Parliament he was appointed a Lord of the Treasury in Sir Robert Peel's government of 1841-46 with its powerful statesmen — Wellington, Stanley, Aberdeen, Goderich, Hardinge, Ellenby, Dalhousie and Canning. In 1841 Gladstone was appointed Vice President of the Board of Trade and Master of the Mint and in 1843 he was President

151

of the Board of Trade. In 1844 he led the Railway Bill through the House of Commons — the 'Parliamentary' train fare was a penny a mile for third class and the train had to exceed a speed of twelve miles per hour. The great engineers — Joseph Locke, George Hudson, Robert Stephenson (son of the great George Stephenson), and Isambard Kingdom Brunel could continue to push ahead with their new railways and civil engineering projects.

Four ministries had fallen since 1852 and Gladstone, to pacify the Peelites, was appointed Chancellor of the Exchequer but he had to struggle with his conscience to serve under Palmerston.

Gladstone's budget of 1853 was masterly — he got rid of 140 duties and lowered another 150, and, in his belief that income tax was evil, he cut it to seven pence in the pound with the intention of reducing it to zero within seven years. In 1865 his budget reduced income tax to four pence, halved the tea duty and reduced expenditure from £72 million to £66 million. He created the Post Office Savings Bank and reiterated his preference to avoid State interference with the maxim that 'God most helps those who help themselves'. He was the power behind the University Act of 1854 which abolished closed fellowships and closed scholarships; he allowed the government of universities by their teachers, opened their halls of residence to men of poorer means and reduced the requirement to take Holy Orders.

In 1868, with the people shouting 'Gladstone and liberty', he formed his first Ministry with a majority of 112 — this Government lasted until 1874 during which the 1870 Education Act was passed and the Acts of Reform he passed met many of the demands of earlier Liberalism. Disestablishment of the Irish Church took place; he abolished Church rates, religious tests for entry to Oxford and Cambridge and the purchase of army commissions (in 1871). He legislated on Irish land and on Education in England and Scotland. He opened the Civil Service to entrance by competitive examination and scrutiny by an independent commission; he made capital relatively safe for the investor by introducing limited liability and trade finance.

In 1874 he dissolved Parliament and lost the subsequent election to his old rival Disraeli which pleased the Queen who much preferred his courtly concern to the stern and austere Gladstone. When Disraeli put through the Royal Titles Bill of 1876 describing the Queen as Empress of India, Gladstone opposed it as 'flummery'. There were times when the Queen came near to open hatred and undisguised enmity of Gladstone; she used all her influence against him and he, in turn, did nothing to assuage her. But Gladstone, by no means beaten, became Prime Minister again in 1880. Five years later the Irish problem contributed to his resignation. During his election campaign *The Scotsman* of 18th June 1886 reported:

> It is estimated that between 40,000 and 50,000 people assembled on Waverley Bridge and in Princes Street to receive the Premier on his arrival, and the enthusiasm of this assemblage knew no bounds.

He returned to the Premiership for the third time and, with the same, apparently inexhaustible supply of energy, at the age of seventy-five, he tried again to get the Home Rule for Ireland Bill through Parliament but it just failed.

In 1892 Gladstone, ageing, half blind and partially deaf, formed his last Government. It was a sorry business; he could not withstand the pressures of Cabinet dissension; one faction, the Imperialists, wanted to keep Uganda and Egypt, the others, old Radicals, thought this tyrannical but Gladstone remained single-minded about Irish Home Rule while the country was plagued with strikes. His Irish Bill got through the Commons but failed miserably in the Lords — this was the end of Gladstone's political life. He resigned in March 1894 and retired, with approbation from both sides of the House, to write his memoirs in Wales. He died aged eighty-nine in 1898 and was buried in Westminster.

By continuing along the main street to Shandwick Place you will reach the West End and Princes Street which marks the end of this tour walk.

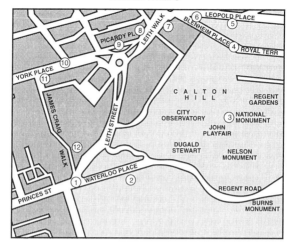

Capital Walk 3

1 Waterloo Place
2 Old Calton Burial Ground
3 Calton Hill
4 Royal Terrace
5 Leopold Place
6 Blenheim Place
7 Baxter's Place
8 Union Place
9 Picardy Place
10 York Place
11 Elder Street
12 St James Centre

1 Waterloo Place

This was designed by Archibald Elliot in the year of the great victory over the French — the Battle of Waterloo — 1815. The engineer was Robert Stevenson, grandfather of Robert Louis Stevenson. Elliot also designed the Regent Bridge over Calton Road below; it was opened by Prince Leopold in 1819. Waterloo, ten miles south of Brussels, was Wellington's chosen location for his last stand against the French and his victory on 18th June 1815 brought to an end the Napoleonic War.

2 Old Calton Burial Ground

Situated on the right-hand-side of Waterloo Place, contains several interesting memorials: The Political Martyr's Monument, David Hume Monument, the Emancipation Monument, the grave of Daniel Stewart and many others.

The obelisk by Thomas Hamilton, the Martyr's Monument is inscribed:

> To the memory of Thomas Muir, Thomas Fyshe Palmer, Maurice Margarot and Joseph Gerald. Erected by friends of Parliamentary Reform in England and Scotland. 1844

The trial of **Thomas Muir** (1765-98) became a 'cause célèbre' in Britain, France and America. This brilliant young advocate's only crime was to preach for reform; he was sentenced to fourteen years transportation to Botany Bay in 1793 and he was rescued by the American Navy. After many adventures he died of his wounds in France.

The monument to **David Hume** (1711-76) was designed by Robert Adam and erected in 1777. David Hume was Britain's greatest living philosopher and historian — his History of England, the first to be written, was an unrivalled masterpiece. The University of Edinburgh named one of its tower blocks in George Square after him.

The Emancipation Monument is the Scottish

American Soldiers' Memorial with the bronze statue of Abraham Lincoln (1809-65), the 16th President of USA who abolished slavery and brought his torn country through a cruel civil war only to be assassinated on Good Friday, 14th April 1865.

The grave of **Daniel Stewart** (1741-1814) is at the south end of the burial ground. He was the founder of Daniel Stewart's Hospital, now Daniel Stewart's and Melville College in Queensferry Road. He was a valet to a rich merchant in India who left him £11,000 in 1760 (about £1.5 million today). Stewart returned to Edinburgh and lived carefully, in fact he took a humble job as a macer at £50 a year. He doubled his inheritance for the erection of the hospital.

3 Calton Hill

On the left side of the steps leading to the Calton hill is the 'Rock House' wrought-iron gate — the entrance to the home and studio of a pioneer of the art of photography, David Octavius Hill (1800-48) who became a Royal Scottish Academician. His work is a lasting record of subjects such as the stone-masons of the Scott Monument in Princes Street, the fishwives of Newhaven and the churchmen of the 'Disruption' of 1843.

From the top of Calton Hill the view north is over the Firth of Forth to the kingdom of Fife beyond, to the south is the extinct volcano Arthur's Seat with Salisbury Crags and the Royal residence of Holyroodhouse with the Burns Monument immediately below in Regent Road. Facing west the view is over Princes Street, the New Town and Edinburgh Castle.

The monuments on Calton Hill are the National Monument, Nelson's Monument, the John Playfair Monument and Dugald Stewart's Monument. **The City Observatory** was designed in 1818 by William H. Playfair for his uncle, Professor John Playfair, who was the President of the Astronomical Institution founded in 1812.

The National Monument by W.H. Playfair and C.R. Cockerell was designed as a facsimile of the Parthenon in Athens to commemorate the dead of the Napoleonic War but it was never completed due to lack of public subscription.

The Nelson Monument by Robert Burn in 1907 commemorates Admiral Lord Nelson (1758-1805) the victor of the great sea-battle of Trafalgar in 1805. Nelson, the inspiration to the British Navy, lost his right eye at Corsica, his right arm at Tenerife and his life at Trafalgar. The three bands on the collar of all sailors of the Royal Navy represent Nelson's most famous victories — the Nile, Copenhagen and Trafalgar.

The Dugald Stewart Monument is the circular, colonnaded design of W.H. Playfair of 1831 and commemorates possibly the most popular teacher of philosophy of the University of Edinburgh. He was Professor of Moral Philosophy and a luminary of the Scottish Enlightenment. He died in 1828 almost at the close of the 'Golden Age'.

The John Playfair Monument was designed by his nephew W.H. Playfair in 1825-26. John Playfair (1748-1819) was the first President of the Astronomical Institution and Professor of Mathematics of the University of Edinburgh. He was appointed Professor of Natural Philosophy and was probably best known for his support of James Hutton's work in his *Illustrations of the Huttonian Theory of the Earth* which led to the recognition of the science of Geology and to James Hutton as its father.

A curious discovery recently by a Canadian potholer was the existence of a stone-vaulted tomb adjacent to the north wall of the City Observatory. It has been ascertained that this is the grave of a well respected Jewish dentist and chiropodist, Herman Lyon, who died about 1800.

Looking south over the Queen's Park, immediately below is the **Burns Monument** commemorating Scotland's national bard, Robert Burns (1759-96).

4   Royal Terrace

Having walked over Calton Hill to its north side we reach W.H. Playfair's superb design of Royal Terrace, named to commemorate the Royal visit of 1822 by George IV — the first monarch to visit Scotland since Charles II in 1650.

5   *Leopold Place*

Another of Playfair's designs, Leopold Place can be seen across the gardens of London Road. It is named after King Leopold of the Belgians (1790-1865) who with his wife Princess Charlotte, daughter of George IV, was a great favourite in Britain. He opened the Regent Bridge in Waterloo Place in 1819.

6   *Blenheim Place*

Turning left towards Leith Walk we reach Blenheim Place which commemorates the Duke of Marlborough's victory at the Battle of Blenheim in 1704 which saved Vienna, drove the French back to the Rhine and effectively ended Louis XIV's reign.

7   *Baxter's Place*

This is named after the architect John Baxter who feued this part of the main street in 1780. Nos.1-3 were the home and office of the famous lighthouse engineer, Robert Stevenson who designed and built lighthouses around the Scottish coast; he also engineered roadways, bridges, harbours and many other works. He was the grandfather of the famous novelist, Robert Louis Stevenson.

8   *Union Place*

Lying across Leith Street, Union Place commemorates the Union of Ireland with Britain on 1st January 1801. It ended with Irish Partition in 1920-22 brought about by the Irish Home Rule movement.

9   *Picardy Place*

Derives its name from the French district of Picardy from whence the refugee Protestant Huguenots fled after Louis XIV revoked the Edict of Nantes of 1598 in 1685. Picardy Place was the birthplace of Sir Arthur

Conan Doyle (1859-1930) who created the fictional detective, Sherlock Holmes. The statue by Gerald Laing of Holmes in Picardy Place, was unveiled in June 1991. Arthur Conan Doyle graduated MD from the University of Edinburgh and wrote his mysteries simply to augment his income as a doctor in London. Such was the expertise of his analysis he was consulted by police forces in England, France and China. Regrettably, his advice was occasionally wrong!

10 York Place

The continuation of Picardy Place, is named after 'The noble Duke of York' — Frederick (1763-1827), the second son of George III. He was appointed Commander-in-Chief of the British Army in 1798 but his success was in reorganising the army rather than in winning battles. His amours caught up with him and after an enquiry relating to the sale of commissions he was exonerated but unpopular.

No.32 York Place, Raeburn House, was the studio of Sir Henry Raeburn (1756-1823) the Scottish portrait painter who was famous for his character portraits. He was knighted during George IV's visit to Scotland in 1822. He was appointed His Majesty's Limner shortly before he died.

11 Elder Street

Almost opposite Raeburn House is Elder Street of which very little is left; it is named after Thomas Elder (1737-99) who was twice Lord Provost of Edinburgh during the French Revolution. He actively suppressed any person or group, such as the 'Friends of the People', thought to be sympathetic to the revolutionary cause. He pressed strongly for the rebuilding of the 'tounis college' (University of Edinburgh) of which his son-in-law, George Baird, became Principal.

12 St James Centre

Passing the Bus Station and New St Andrews House we arrive at St James Centre — a large shopping precinct which takes its name from the demolished St James Square surreptitiously named after the 'Old Pretender', James Francis Edward Stuart. The King James Hotel is named after him although he was never king. His uprising in 1715 was a failure as was his son's attempt to gain the crown for his father in 1745. He would have been James VIII of Scotland and III of England had the rebellion succeeded.

Biographical histories

WATERLOO PLACE LOOKING TOWARDS CALTON HILL

1   Waterloo Place

The Wellington statue in front of Register House in Princes Street faces south but the 'Iron Duke' on horseback has his arm extended pointing east to Waterloo Place which is the triumphal access to the east from Princes Street. It was designed in 1815 by Archibald Elliot and the engineer was Robert Stevenson. Its twin fluted Ionic porticos form a superb frame for the view of Nelson's monument on Calton Hill.

The Regent Bridge, also by Elliot, with its Ionic colonnades and Corinthian columns in the central arch, spans Calton Road below; the inscription on the south side reads:

> Opened August 18th 1819 for entry of His Royal Highness Prince Leopold of Saxe-Coburg

and that on the north side:

> Commenced in the ever memorable year 1815. Sir John Marjoribanks of Lees, Baronet MP Lord Provost of the City. Archibald Elliot, Architect.

The great, but hard won, victory of the Battle of Waterloo on 18th June 1815 brought to an end the Napoleonic Wars. The hero was the British Commander-in-Chief, the Duke of Wellington.

Just as it seemed that peace in Europe had been achieved, the allies, having signed the Treaty of Paris with Louis XVIII (and Napoleon having abdicated to Elba), started quarrelling amongst themselves over boundaries. An army of a million French soldiers was very suspicious of the Bourbon throne supported by their recent enemies.

Prussia threatened war having lost Poland to the Russians and Lord Castlereagh, the British Minister of War, took on his greatest responsibility by signing a secret treaty with Austria and France against a Prussian attack. On the same day that Castlereagh returned to England, Napoleon landed in the south of France — the 1st March 1815. Louis XVIII fled when his army deserted him to support Napoleon who struck quickly, knowing that the British were weak after the American war.

Wellington had 67,000 men of which one third were British; they were thinly stretched from Ostend to Liége (150 miles/240km) and Napoleon attacked their centre at Charleroi, thirty miles south of Brussels and on the 16th June he advanced to the north east. Wellington had to retreat on the 17th to join the Prussians on whom he depended for support. The Duke however, had planned exactly where he would take his stand; he knew every ridge, valley and woodland around the little village of Waterloo, ten miles to the south of Brussels in the middle of the forest of Soignies. He placed 17,000 men ten miles north-west at Hal, in case Napoleon tried a turning movement. Napoleon, too sure of himself, assumed that the Prussians had given up in retreat after their defeat at Ligny and he sent 30,000 men to follow them, losing valuable time and manpower in the process.

At Waterloo the French had 74,000 men and 246 guns; Wellington had 7,000 men less and 184 guns. He knew that this would be a close run battle. It was Sunday, 18th June 1815, a dull, wet day. The artillery of both sides opened fire just before noon and at 4.30pm the tough, crude Prussian Prince Blücher attacked the French right and another Prussian corps supported the

British on their left. The French Field Marshal Ney led his cavalry to the centre prematurely and was beaten back by bayonet and a fusillade of fire. On his second attack he broke through the allied line to be met by a Prussian column. Other Prussian columns, supporting the British left, gave Wellington his opportunity to rip open Napoleon's centre. Ney's guards fought their last bitter battle and Wellington ordered a general advance. The French were routed and the Battle of Waterloo ended the dreams of Emperor Napoleon. The allies lost 21,000 men of which 15,000 were British. The French lost 25,000 and many thousands more were taken prisoner.

2 Old Calton Burial Ground

In the Old Calton Burial Ground, off Waterloo Place, the tall Cleopatra's needle, the obelisk by Thomas Hamilton, commemorates the **Political Martyrs** of 1793. The inscription on its base reads:

> To the memory of Thomas Muir, Thomas Fyshe Palmer, William Skirving, Maurice Margarot and Joseph Gerald. Erected by friends of Parliamentary Reform in England and Scotland. 1844.

This was during Pitt's 'Reign of Terror' between 1792-94. France had declared war and there was great fear, especially in Scotland, of riot and sedition. Henry Dundas 'ruled' Scotland with an iron hand; many were sent to the gallows or transported to Botany Bay.

The trial of **Thomas Muir** caused a furore throughout Scotland. He had offended the 1792 proclamation against seditious writing. He was put on trial before the feared Lord Braxfield having been arrested for sedition. The Prosecutor was Robert Dundas, a nephew of the despotic Henry Dundas. Even the jury shuddered before the wrathful scorn of Braxfield's waspish tongue. There was no evidence against Muir, the brilliant young advocate who defended himself. The prosecution had singularly failed to prove any crime but the jury, badgered and directed by Braxfield, found him guilty little realising what they had done. He was sentenced to fourteen years deportation to Botany Bay — for what? The jurors, ashamed and frightened, went into hiding for fear of attack. Years later one of them was heard to remark: 'We were all mad that day'.

Thomas Muir was born on 24th August 1765, his father, Thomas Muir, was a successful tradesman who sent his only son to Glasgow Grammar School and then to the University. Young Thomas quickly developed a political awareness and was expelled from the university for lampooning those professors who had quarrelled with his hero, Professor John Anderson. Anderson was sympathetic with the cause of the French uprising and he had devised an ingenious way of smuggling French newspapers to Germany — he attached them to small balloons and waited for a favourable wind to carry them

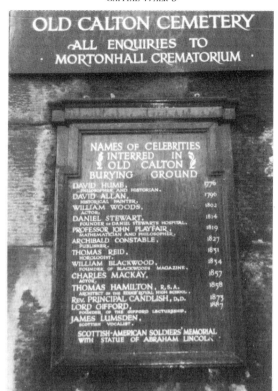

across the border. The Anderson Institute, now Strathclyde University, was named after him.

Thomas Muir continued his studies at the University of Edinburgh and he was admitted to the Faculty of Advocates on 24th November 1787. He became an elder of Cadder Church near Glasgow and sat in the General Assembly of the Church of Scotland. At the Bar he had established a reputation as a good orator and had defended many poor and oppressed people for no fee.

He had become a prominent member of the Friends of the People, a society established in July 1792 and Muir advocated and agitated for parliamentary reform — votes for all over the age of twenty-one. He attended meetings of the London Society of Friends of the People at Kirkintilloch and Milton and at the Convention in Edinburgh he read an address from the United Irishmen. The climate for reform seemed perfect; the French had stormed the Bastille only three years before (July 1789), by 1791 it seemed that the whole of Europe would rise in revolt and the French threatened war against their neighbours. Prime Minister Pitt responded with his 'reign of terror' (1792-94), well supported by Dundas and Braxfield, against anyone suspected of sympathy for the French.

After Muir's arrest, on 2nd January 1793, he refused to answer the Sheriff's questions and he was released on bail to be shunned and insulted by his fellow advocates. He left for France having been commissioned by the London Society to plead for the life of Louis XVI, but he arrived in Paris the day after he had been guillotined. He was given a warm welcome in Paris but meanwhile, in Edinburgh, he had been declared an outlaw and was struck off the roll of the Faculty of Advocates.

On his return to Scotland he was arrested on 30th August and charged with 'exciting a spirit of disloyalty and disaffection, of recommending Paine's Rights of Man, of distributing seditious writings and of reading aloud a seditious writing.' He had asked the skilled and popular Henry Erskine to defend him but, when Erskine quite correctly insisted on conducting the case without interference, Muir decided to defend himself. This was no doubt a mistake as Henry Erskine was held in great esteem and highly respected, even by Judge Braxfield. Muir firstly objected to five of the fifteen jurors on the grounds that they were members of the Goldsmiths' Assocation which had offered a reward for the apprehension of anyone found to be circulating the works of Thomas Paine. Braxfield, with an imperious wave, dismissed the objection as nonsense. Muir called witnesses who confirmed his deprecation of violence and that his visit to France was simply intended to save life. The conduct of the trial was biased against Muir from the start. It finished at 2.00am on the 31st August 1793 and at noon on that day, Muir was found guilty and sentenced to fourteen years transportation to Botany Bay. The jurymen were aghast; there had been no case to answer and they had delivered the verdict through fear — one of them having received an anonymous, threatening letter. Both Houses of Parliament disputed the legality of the sentence, but to no avail.

Muir, with his co-accused Palmer, Skirving, Margarot and Gerald were transported to Botany Bay in March 1794. Muir bought a farm which he named Hunter's Hill after his grandmother's family; it is now a suburb of Sydney. This total disregard for justice created uproar not only in Scotland but in the United States of America where it was decided to rescue Muir — a ship was sent to Australia and Muir

THE DAVID HUME MONUMENT WITH THE POLITICAL MARTYRS' MONUMENT, BELOW

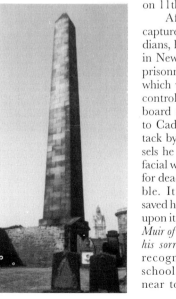

sailed out of Botany Bay on 11th February 1796.

After shipwreck, capture by American Indians, hospital treatment in New Mexico and imprisonment at Havanah which was under British control, he was sent on board a Spanish frigate to Cadiz. During an attack by two English vessels he received a severe facial wound and was left for dead clutching his bible. It was this which saved him; the inscription upon it, *To my son, Thomas Muir of Hunter's Hill, from his sorrowing mother*, was recognised by an old school friend. He was near to death and had

169

lost one eye and half his face. His friend took him ashore but when his wounds had been tended he was arrested by the Spanish. The French Directory obtained his release and offered him hospitality and citizenship. He was given a public reception at Bordeaux and a warm welcome in Paris on 4th September 1798. His wounds worsened and he lived for only another seven months. He died at Chantilly on 27th September 1798, aged thirty-three years — an event which saddened the whole of Scotland.

The author Robert Louis Stevenson wittily described David Hume's monument in the Old Calton Burial ground thus:

> *Within this circular idea, called vulgarly a tomb, The impressions and Ideas rest, That constituted Hume.*

Hume's monument is the finest in the cemetery. It was designed by Robert Adam and was erected in 1777, one year after his death. **David Hume** was Scotland's, if not Britain's, greatest philosopher and historian whose influence spread over the whole of the Western World. He devoted his life to the study of philosophy and was the first to write a complete and definitive history of England. He was the leading light of the 'Golden Age' (1760-90). He was not a reclusive inhabitant of an ivory tower but a gregarious man who loved company, revelled in discussion and enjoyed a good argument.

He made his first home, in 1751, in Riddles Court which is on the south side of Lawnmarket; he then moved to Jack's land at 229 Canongate, to James Court in 1769 and finally to St David Street in 1771 where he died.

Born in Edinburgh on 26th April 1711; his family is a branch of the Earl of Home or Hume on his father's side and his mother was the daughter of Sir David Falconer, President of the Court of Justice; her brother succeeded to the title of Lord Halkerton.

Hume's childhood in Berwickshire was one of strict Calvinism and at an early stage of his life he was 'seized with a passion for literature', a passion he never lost. At the age of eleven years he was sent to the University of Edinburgh for about four years. His family considered that law was a proper profession for him but his aversion to studies other than philosophy led him secretly to Cicero and Virgil instead of Voet and Vinnius.

David Hume was not one of those whose family could afford to send him on the grand tour of Europe complete with tutor. In 1734 lack of money forced him to find a job in Bristol but he gave this up as soon as he had sufficient money to take him to Reims in France where his aim was to improve his knowledge of literature. At La Flêche in Anjou he wrote his famous *Treatise of Human Nature* and after three happy years he returned to London to publish it in 1738 — it was not successful. Undeterred, he had it printed in Edinburgh and followed it with the first part of his *Essays Moral, Political and Literary* — this was an immediate success. Reading it today, it is still modern, still relevant. For example:

> It is evident that every man loves himself better than any other person, he is naturally impelled to extend his acquisitions as much as possible; and nothing can restrain him in this propensity but reflection and experience, by which he learns the pernicious effects of that licence, and the total dissolution of society which must ensue from it.

At the invitation of the Marquess of Annandale he became his tutor but only tolerated it for a year in England. He then became Secretary and aide-de-camp to General St Clair and he travelled with him to France, Vienna and Turin. During this two-year interruption to his studies he lived frugally, saved £1000 and re-wrote his *Treatise on Human Nature*, renaming it *The Enquiry of Human Understanding*. This version was only slightly more successful. In 1749, while living with his brother, he wrote the second part of his essays *Political Discourses*, and his *Enquiry concerning the Principles of Morals*. Meantime his Edinburgh bookseller found that his former publications were being widely discussed and new editions were demanded.

In 1751 he moved back to Edinburgh to live at Riddles Court where he started work on his *History of England*. Within a year his *Political Discourses* was published with immediate success. This puzzled him as he always considered that his *Enquiry concerning the Princi-*

ples of Morals was his best work. He was then appointed Librarian to the Faculty of Advocates in 1752. This gave him access to a great library and led him to plan the writing of the *History of England*, commencing with the House of Stuart. His first of six volumes was criticised because he had shown sympathy for the fate of Charles I and the Earl of Stratford. The book sank into oblivion. It was, however, the first of its kind; no one had ever undertaken such a task before.

In 1756 Hume, ignoring public opinion, published the second volume of his *History of England*. It dealt with the period from the death of Charles I to the Revolution and was deemed acceptable by the Whigs, but Hume, ignoring their opinions, published his *History of the House of Tudor*. The outburst of anger against it equalled that against his first volume, but this was the raving of political self-interest. By 1762 he had completed all six volumes — a mammoth task, an unrivalled masterpiece.

In 1763, after a second invitation from the Earl of Hertford, Hume accepted the post of Secretary to the Embassy in Paris. After two years he became Chargé d'Affaires until the arrival of the Duke of Richmond. He left Paris in 1766 and returned to Edinburgh in a considerably improved financial state. He had intended to have a short sabbatical, but in 1767 he was appointed an Under-Secretary of State in London. Two years later he returned again to Edinburgh, a considerably richer man, to live in James Court, off Lawnmarket. His next residence was at elegant St Andrew Square which had just been built preceding James Craig's New Town plan.

Hume was now in great demand, his reputation was established and he became one of the leaders of the literati. Edinburgh abounded with clubs whose members discussed, debated and analysed in microscopic detail every aspect of philosophy and science. This was the centre of intellectual stimulation in Europe for what came to be called the 'Scottish Enlightenment'. David Hume was one of many men to whom the King's Chemist, Mr Amyat, referred when he lived in Edinburgh, 'Here I stand at what is called the 'Cross of Edinburgh', and can, in a few minutes, take fifty men of genius and learning by the hand.'

Whilst at St Andrew Square — he lived in the house at the south west corner — Miss Nancy Orde, daughter of Baron Orde, had the name St David painted on the corner wall as a mischievous allusion to Hume's agnosticism. It was at St Andrew Square that Hume enjoyed the company of many old acquaintances, friends and distinguished visitors. One in the latter category was Benjamin Franklin when he was given the Freedom of the City in 1768. In a letter to his old friend, Adam Smith, we gain a glimpse of their jovial and challenging relationship:

> I want to know what you have been doing, and propose to exact a rigorous account of the method in which you have employed yourself during your Retreat. I am positive you are wrong in many of your speculations especially where you have the misfortune to differ from me — I expect to find a letter from you containing a bold acceptance of this defiance.

Hume and Smith were members of the Poker Club (founded in 1762) the original aim of which was to revive the Scottish Militia disbanded after the '45 Rebellion, but which developed into an intellectual forum for the intelligentsia of Edinburgh.

In retirement he spent much of his time revising the histories and he wrote his *Dialogues Concerning Natural Religion*, but he did not live to hear the renewed outrage against him. The General Assembly of the Church of Scotland had already tried to have him expelled in 1756 for his scepticism and irreligion. In his *Dialogues*, Hume's scepticism attacked the accepted conception of God and in his essay *On Miracles*, he asserted that 'no testimony for any kind of miracle has ever amounted to a probability, much less a proof'.

Hume became ill in 1775 and completed *My Own Life* on which much of this short account is based. The great man died on Sunday 25th August 1776 after a long illness during which he was attended at his house in St David Street by Dr Joseph Black, scientist, academic and physician. 'Britain had lost its greatest and most influential philosopher; he had challenged the world with his new ideas of human nature in the formation of judgements and in the acquisition of knowledge.'

The Emancipation Monument is the Scottish-American Soldiers' Memorial, with the bronze statue of American President Abraham Lincoln who is looked upon by a freed slave, was sculpted by George E. Bissell in 1893. The lifesize monument, the first in Europe of an American President, commemorates the five Scottish-Americans who fought in the American Civil War of 1861 during which Lincoln freed the slaves and at the end of which he was assassinated.

Daniel Stewart's grave is prominent at the south end of the Old Calton Burial Ground. He was the founder of Daniel Stewart's Hospital — now Daniel Stewart's and Melville College. This independent school was created from the amalgamation of the two schools and is accommodated in the Daniel Stewart's building in Queensferry Road. This stately structure of turrets and towers is a combination of Jacobean and Elizabethan design by David Rhind, in 1848, who used W.H. Playfair's design of Donaldson's Hospital as the basis of his submission to the trustees.

Daniel Stewart's College opened its doors to fifty boys, chosen from seventy-six, in 1855. Preference was given to poor boys named Stewart or Macfarlane. Melville College was originally called the Edinburgh Institution for Languages and Mathematics. It opened on 1st October 1832 in No.59 George Street and moved to Hill Street after one year where it remained for the next twenty years. Its next destination was Queen Street and then, in 1920, new school buildings in Melville Street were found and in 1936 the governors decided to change its name to that of its new address — Melville College.

Daniel Stewart (1741-1814) made no political impact on Scotland; he gained his fortune from a fortuitous inheritance, whereas Melville was the 1st Viscount Melville, Henry Dundas, (1742-1811) whose biography is covered in Capital Walk 1, number 25 on page 86.

Daniel Stewart was born in Logierait, a few miles south of Pitlochry, in 1741. His crofter father put young Daniel to work as a herd boy but he became bored with this lonely occupation and decided to try his luck in the city. He found work as an apprentice wigmaker and enjoyed chatting with the customers. His personality gained him favour with a very rich merchant who was visiting his home from India and who had the idea that a young man from Scotland with such an obliging personality would make an excellent valet. Young Daniel was completely taken aback when he was invited to fill the post and, having taken the great step from Logierait to Edinburgh, he decided to risk the giant leap to India. He was one of those Highland lads who was completely dependable and served his master with efficiency and pride. Within a few years his master took ill and died and Daniel had an even greater surprise; in his Will his employer had left him the princely sum of £11,000 (about £1.5 million today).

Daniel Stewart returned to Edinburgh and instead of living up to his huge inheritance he invested it and took a humble position as a Macer to the Court of the Exchequer with a salary of £50 per year. His duties required that he carried the mace before the judge as he entered and left the court. He attended juries, took charge of witnesses and swore in those who made affidavits. At first he lived near David Hume in Lawnmarket and in 1784 he moved house to Crighton's Entry in the Canongate until finally, in 1793, he took a house in Windmill Street where he employed a housekeeper to look after his invalid niece.

In 1800 he was appointed Depute Court Marshal; his salary was increased to £80 per year and his duties included taking charge of the prisoners in court. He commissioned Henry Raeburn to paint his portrait for one hundred guineas (£105) and paid him promptly. Raeburn remarked 'It would be a great deal in my pocket if everybody was as anxious to be out of debt as you are'.

His life was quite uneventful and after forty-three years service he died on 14th May 1814 and was buried at the Old Calton Burial Ground. In his Will he appended a note which gives an indication of his careful nature: 'There will be little or no debts after my death, because I pay ready money for everthing I buy … and I pay tradespeople I employ for repairing my properties when the work is done, I recommend it to my trustees to do the same and the work will be done well and cheaper'. He left a life rent to his niece, Isabella Stewart, to whom he was devoted but he left nothing to his housekeeper because she had a sharp tongue and had been unkind to his niece.

His original investment of £11,000 had almost doubled and he directed his general testamentary trustees to accumulate his estate of money and property until it reached the sum of £40,000 before proceeding with the erection of a Hospital — 'the absorbing dream of his existence'. When his niece died, in 1845, the trustees had accumulated £80,000 and the building of Daniel Stewart's Hospital began in 1849. In 1953 the former pupils gave a generous gift of £2,000 for a library in memory of their founder and, as a further memorial his portrait was presented to the school by Bailie Tom Curr.

3   Calton Hill

The monuments on Calton Hill are: **Dugald Stewart** by William H. Playfair in 1831 and modelled on the choragic Monument of Lysicrates of Athens; John Playfair again by WH Playfair (his nephew) in 1825-26 in the style of Lion Tomb at Cnidos (without the lions); **The National Monument** commemorates the dead of the Napoleonic War by W.H. Playfair and C.R. Cockerell. It was intended to be 'a facsimile of the Parthenon' but was left unfinished in 1829 due to lack of public subscription; **Admiral Lord Nelson** by Robert Burn in 1807 — built two years after the Battle of Trafalgar. In the 1850s a time-ball was installed at the top of the monument and on 5th June 1861 the drop of the time-ball was synchronised with the firing of a cannon at precisely 1.00 pm at the Castle.

There are two buildings on Calton Hill the first of which is the **City Observatory**. This was designed in 1818 by W.H. Playfair for the Astronomical Institution founded six years before. The architect's uncle, Professor John Playfair, was the Institution's first president.

The Observatory House on the south-west corner was built for an optician-astronomer, Robert Short, and started in 1776 but lack of funds caused its postponement until 1788 when the City fathers appointed James Craig, the medal-winning New Town architect, to complete the work in the style of a Gothic-towered fortification

The National Monument

The Napoleonic War had ended in 1815; Scotland had sacrificed thousands of men in the prime of their lives. Seven years had passed, King George IV, had visited Scotland and it seemed to such eminent men as Sir Walter Scott, Lord Cockburn and Lord Elgin that there should be a proper memorial to those who had sacrificed their lives, that such a memorial should be in the Capital City and that it should be situated in a most prominent place — Calton Hill. In 1822 a number of subscribers including Scott, Cockburn and Elgin appealed for £42,000 and planned a National Monument and 'intended it to be an exact model of the Parthenon in Athens, and to commemorate the heroes who fell at Waterloo'.

W.H. Playfair and C.R. Cockerell were commissioned to design the Monument. Money was slow to come in. The citizens of Edinburgh gave generously but the rest of Scotland was not sufficiently interested in so lavish a memorial and of course times were hard in the 1820s after a costly war. Only about half the money was raised and work began in 1826. Twelve columns in Craigleith stone were completed of what would have been a temple as a church.

On 30th June 1829 Playfair wrote to Cockerell, 'Our Parthenon is come to a dead halt, and is, I am afraid, likely to stand up a striking proof of the pride and poverty of us Scots … Wallace's contract is finished, and what is to be done next I know not. I suppose, Nothing!'

Nelson's Monument

The neo-Gothic tower on Calton Hill, Nelson's Columm, designed in 1907 by Robert Burn in the shape of an inverted telescope, is an unmistakable landmark in Edinburgh which, on more than one occasion, has been threatened with demolition.

Nelson Street and monument commemorate Admiral Horatio Nelson, the famous naval hero of many victories culminating with his last — the Battle of Trafalgar in 1805 in which he died of wounds and before which he sent the famous signal to action — 'England expects every man will do his duty'. Nelson was an inspiration to the British Navy; in the Mediterranean under Lord Hood, at St Vincent under Jervis and at the victory of the Nile.

Nelson was born (the sixth child) on 29th September 1758 in Norfolk; his father was the Rector of Burnham Thorpe. His mother died, aged forty-two (having borne eleven children), when Nelson was nine years old and from then on his father's discipline was strict — he considered it an act of self indulgence if a child's back touched the back of a chair and weak eyes were no excuse for wearing glasses.

Horatio was educated at the Royal Grammar School, Norwich. He was twelve years and three months old when he went to sea as a midshipman on the Raisonable commanded by his uncle, Captain Maurice Suckling. By 1777 he had served on six ships, in the West Indies and on a North Pole expedition where he presented himself for his Lieutenant's examination aged eighteen. He passed easily and without the examiners of the Navy Board knowing that his uncle was its Comptroller — he wanted no favouritism. He received his first commission as Second Lieutenant of the frigate Lowestoffe the following day. A clever start to a naval career considering that the minimum age for entry was twenty years of age. Captain Locker of the Lowestoffe gave Nelson command of a prize he had boarded and with Locker's encouragement he was quickly promoted. When Locker retired, through ill health, Nelson promised that he would always write to him — a promise he faithfully kept.

He was promoted to Post-Captain and served with distinction in Jamaica suffering nightmarish conditions in the tropics of San Juan as commander — only ten out of two hundred of his men survived from disease on the Hinchingbrooke. Nelson himself was very ill and was nursed by the Admiral's lady. In 1781 he was recalled to commission the Abermarl' — a conversion from a captured French merchantman to a 24-gun frigate. It was a 'brute to handle' but nevertheless, from Quebec he joined Lord Hood in New York off Staten Island where he almost gave up a promising naval career to marry the Provost Marshal's dazzlingly beautiful sixteen-year-old daughter.

After his first attendance at Court he spent six months in France but could not master the language. At a time of high unemployment amongst naval officers Nelson managed, through his friends, the Grenvilles, the Lyttletons and the Pitts, to get an appointment to the Boreas and he set sail for the Leeward Islands. He was not impressed by the conditions on the Leewards where trouble greeted him. Firstly, he told the Commissioner that he could not agree to obey any order until he was properly commissioned; next he discovered that the Admiral, Sir Richard Hughes, had been easily swayed into waiving the Navigation Laws for the vessels of the United States. This suited the planters, merchants and the Custom House officials but Nelson firmly enforced the law and found himself ostracised and sued by ship owners. He had to confine himself on board the Boreas for two months to evade arrest.

In 1787, in Charlestown, he fell in love with and married 'dear Fanny' the young widow of Dr Nisbet of Nevis who had a five year old son. She was given away by Prince William and they returned to England, she in a merchant ship and he in his frigate. Nelson became very ill on the journey and was fortunate to survive. He retired to Burnham Thorpe in Norfolk for the next five years on half pay at eight shillings per day. Out of favour at the Admiralty he could not get an appointment; life was unbearable for him and even more so for the ailing Fanny who suffered his frustration.

In 1792 the French revolutionaries declared war on Austria, then Prussia and most of Europe. Napoleon Bonaparte led a brilliant campaign in Italy and an expedition across the Mediterranean to Malta and Egypt. At last in 1793 at the start of the war with France, Nelson was appointed Captain of the Agamemnon and accompanied Lord Hood to the Mediterranean, then to Naples (where he first met Lady Hamilton, wife of the Ambassador) and to the blockade of Corsica. In 1794 Bastia and Calvi were besieged by the naval brigade under his command during which he lost his right eye.

In 1795 he joined Sir William Hotham and gained victories against the French off Toulon. In 1796 the Spanish and French joined forces and Nelson, now a Commodore, was determined that the Spanish fleet would not reach Cadiz; although heavily outgunned he disobeyed orders to take the Spaniards by surprise. This was the famous victory of Cape St Vincent commanded by Jervis on 14th February 1797. Nelson was promoted to Rear-Admiral and awarded the Cross of the Order of the Bath.

At Santa Cruz, Tenerife, in a forlorn attack on the Spanish his right arm was so severely injured, it had to be amputated. His losses were severe, but in 1798 in Aboukir Bay in Egypt he destroyed the French fleet at great risk by entering a strange harbour without charts. He suffered a head wound but took a monumental victory over Napoleon who was blockaded in Egypt and Syria and had deserted his army claiming that he had ordered Admiral de Brueys into Alexandria. The Battle of the Nile on 1st August 1798 cost the British two hundred killed and seven hundred wounded; the French lost 5,225. Aboukir Island was renamed Nelson's Island and when he returned triumphantly to Naples he was showered with gifts and medals and hailed the greatest hero since Sir Francis Drake. Queen Charlotte gave him a warm welcome and Lady Hamilton, wife of the English ambassador, literally swooned over him;

he, in turn, was totally captivated by her. But the celebrations and honours exhausted him; he longed to be at sea again. George III made him Baron Nelson of the Nile, Parliament gave him a pension of £2,000 per year and he was awarded £10,000 by the East India Company.

In July 1799 he quelled the French inspired Jacobin rebellion in Naples but was criticised by Parliament for breaking an armistice; in gratitude, however, the King of Naples made him Duke of Brontë. He had received orders from the Commander-in-Chief in the Mediterranean, Lord Keith, to take his fleet to the defence of Minorca but, having been inextricably caught up in Neapolitan politics, he refused to obey the order and when it was repeated he sent his second-in-command, Sir John Duckworth, while he controlled the blockade of Malta. He was censured for disobedience. He resigned his command and returned to England overland with Sir William and Lady Hamilton. Lord Keith remarked that 'Lady Hamilton had had command of the Fleet long enough'.

His meeting with his wife was acrimonious and they parted for good in November 1800; his admiration for and behaviour towards Lady Hamilton had become painfully obvious. She had given birth to his daughter, Horatia.

In 1801 Denmark, Sweden and Russia had formed their League of Neutrality and were arming themselves in preparation for an attack against Britain. Nelson was promoted to Vice Admiral of the Blue in 1801 and under Sir Hyde Parker he led the attack on Copenhagen and the Danish fleet. Nelson turned his blind eye to Hyde Parker's signal to withdraw and he defeated the Danes in a tough battle. Armistice was declared after his victory which became peace after the murder of the Czar Paul. Nelson was created a Viscount and succeeded Parker as Commander-in-Chief. For the next two years he defended the English coastline in case of invasion by the French. Napoleon, having seized power in 1799, had, through his aggressive policy, annexed territory in Northern Italy and alarmed Europe's rulers. After he became Emperor in 1804 he led the French armies to swift victories and at Austerlitz in 1805 he attacked the Russian Army winning so convincingly that the British Prime Minister, William Pitt, was heard to say, 'Roll up that map of Europe, it will not be wanted for ten years'.

Britain called upon Nelson once more. In 1803 he was given the Mediterrean command. He blockaded Toulon but after two years of 'cat and mouse', the French Admiral Villeneuve escaped and Nelson chased him to the West Indies before they eventually confronted each other off Cape Trafalgar, south of Cadiz, not far from the Strait of Gibraltar. Nelson had joined his fleet the day before his forty-seventh birthday, on 28th September 1805. His battle plan was to engage the French and Spanish fleet in two lines; Collingwood with the stronger line would attack their rear and Nelson with the other line would prevent their vanguard assisting its rear. To great cheers through the fleet his signal was received: 'England expects every man will do his duty'. Collingwood was brilliant; Nelson went straight into the head of the enemy in the Victory, found a gap and blasted the French on both sides. At the moment of his triumph Nelson was shot; he was carried to the cockpit. He knew he was dying. Captain Hardy reported that fifteen French ships were sunk. Nelson whispered that he had hoped for twenty. 'Now I am satisfied. Thank God I have done my duty', and his last wish: 'Take care of poor Lady Hamilton and Horatia'.

The effect of his death was numbing to seamen and to the British public. His funeral procession on 9th January 1806 stretched from St Paul's Cathedral to the Admiralty. Thirty-one Admirals and a hundred Captains, the Duke of York, the Barons, the regiments of Nelson's campaigns led by the Scots Greys — all accompanied the funeral carriage. The streets were crowded with tearful people but a most touching incident marked the respect of his men who were to furl the colours on the coffin. They deliberately seized the largest of the Victory's flags and tore a piece from it to hold to their chests as a memorial of their greatest Commander.

Playfair Monument & Observatory House

The Playfair Monument on Calton Hill commemorates John Playfair the mathematician and geologist of the University of Edinburgh — an illustrious member of the literati of Edinburgh's

'Golden Age'. His monument is appropriately connected to the City Observatory both of which were designed by his nephew W.H. Playfair. Professor John Playfair was the first President of the Astronomical Institution (founded in 1812) which commissioned the design of the observatory in 1818.

John Playfair was born on 10th March 1748 in Benvie four miles west of Dundee. His father, James Playfair, was minister of the Parish Church of Liff and Benvie and he educated his son at home until he was fourteen years of age. He was then sent to St Andrews University from which he graduated in 1765. The following year, aged eighteen and with the confidence of youth, he applied for the Chair in Mathematics at Marischal College at Aberdeen and was third in the competition. He returned to St Mary's College at St Andrews to study theology and he was licensed by the Scottish Presbytery as a Minister of the Church of Scotland in 1770.

In 1772 he applied for the Chair of Natural Philosophy at St Andrews but his lack of experience and adequate sponsorship resulted in failure. That year his father died and he took over the responsibility for his family. He applied for his father's ministry and was inducted at Liff in August 1773. He resigned this charge to take up the position of tutor to the brothers Ferguson of Raith, one of whom was Sir Ronald Ferguson. During this tutorship, in 1785, he was appointed Joint Professor of Mathematics with Dr Adam Ferguson (who became Sir Adam Ferguson and was son of Professor Adam Ferguson — the 'father' of sociology) at the University of Edinburgh. During this co-professorship he wrote his famous work, the *Elements of Geometry* in 1795 (it reached its eleventh edition in 1859). He had already become a member of the newly founded Royal

Society of Edinburgh (1783) and was its general secretary until his death, twenty-six years later.

When, in 1805, he exchanged his Chair of Mathematics for that of Natural Philosophy he strongly supported the candidature of John Leslie (later Sir John) for the vacancy against the Church. Leslie was a devotee of the great philosopher and historian, David Hume, who was well known for his theological scepticism. Playfair's main work at this time (1812-16) was his *Outlines of Natural Philosophy* and at the end of the war with France in 1815 he travelled through France, Switzerland and Italy to study the geology and minerology of these countries. He greatly admired the work of James Hutton, the acknowledged father of geology and one of Playfair's greatest works, *Illustrations of the Huttonian Theory of the Earth*, helped gain the recognition subsequently given to this science which at that time was a mere branch of chemistry. Playfair spent five years preparing this great work described in *The Dictionary of National Biography* as 'a model of purity of diction, simplicity of style and clearness of explanation. It not only gave popularity to Hutton's work, but helped to create the science of geology'.

Professor John Playfair died in Edinburgh on 20th July 1819. His passing was commented upon by Lord Cockburn in his *Memorials of His Time*:

> This was an irreparable loss to both science and to the society of Edinburgh. Taking the whole man - his science, his heart, his manner, and his taste, I do not see how Playfair could have been improved. Profound, yet cheerful; social yet always respectable; strong in his feelings, but uniformly gentle; a universal favourite, yet never moved from his simplicity; in humble circumstances, but contented and charitable - he realised our ideas of an amiable philosopher. And is he not the best philosophical writer in the English language?

Dugald Stewart Monument

The Dugald Stewart Monument on Calton Hill appears in the foreground of many photographs of Princes Street taken from the Calton Hill. It is the circular, colonnaded, Athenian design (modelled on the monument of Lysicrates of Athens) by W.H.  Playfair in 1831, in memory of one of the many luminaries of the 'Scottish Enlightenment' (1760-90) — an age of intellectual brilliance in Scotland.

Playfair, Edinburgh's celebrated architect, was an admirer of his uncle John Playfair's friend and co-professor of the University of Edinburgh — Dugald Stewart, the Scottish philosopher who was born on 22nd November 1753 in Edinburgh. His father was Matthew Stewart (1717-85) the mathematician. Young Dugald was educated at Glasgow University under Thomas Reid and he became a devotee of Reid's common-sense philosophy.

In 1773, barely twenty, Dugald Stewart read his essay *On Dreaming* to the Speculative Society and two years later he was appointed Assistant in Mathematics under his father's professorship. He was elected Joint-Professor with his father in 1775. He succeeded Adam Ferguson (1723-1816) to the chair of Moral Philosophy in 1785 and proceeded to systemise the doctrines of the Scottish school. He placed psychological matters fully with the philosophy of mind; his lectures were 'sell-outs'; he captivated and inspired his students often causing great sensation in the process. In Cockburn's Memorials he is described as:

> … about middle size, weak limbed, and with an appearance of feebleness which gave an air of delicacy to his gait and structure. His forehead was large and bald, his eyebrows bushy, his eyes grey and intelligent, and capable of conveying any emotion … the voice was singularly pleasing;

a slight burr only made its tones softer. His ear, both for music and for speech was exquisite; and he was the finest reader I have ever heard ... his whole manner was that of an academical gentleman ... Stewart dealt as little as possible with metaphysics, avoided details, and shrank, with a horror which was sometimes rather ludicrous, from all polemical matter. Invisible distinctions, vain contentions, factious theories, philosophical sectarianism, had no attractions for him; and their absence left him free for those moral themes on which he could soar without perplexing his hearers or wasting himself, by useless and painful subtleties ... Stewart was uniformly great and fascinating. Everything was purified and exalted by his beautiful taste ... he breathed the love of virtue into whole generations of pupils.

In 1810 he retired through illness; his able successor was Dr Thomas Brown, but there was genuine sorrow at his loss to the College. Cockburn who was one of his students said, 'we could scarcely bring ourselves to believe that that voice was to be heard no more. The going down of such a luminary cast a foreboding gloom over the friends of mental philosophy, and deprived the College of its purest'.

Dugald Stewart died on 11th June 1828; the end of the 'Golden Age' was approaching. He had suffered from palsy for the last seven years of his life but his mental faculties remained in sparkling form; he corrected and revised the last two volumes of his last book only months before his death. He was buried in the Canongate Churchyard; the service was not public and was attended by magistrates and professors.

Burns Monument

From Calton Hill the view over Queen's Park to the south-east overlooks Holyroodhouse, Salisbury Crags and the extinct volcano of Arthur's Seat; but almost immediately below, on Regent Road, is the Grecian monument to Scotland's greatest poet and songwriter — Robert Burns. It was designed by Thomas Hamilton in 1830.

A statue of Burns can be seen in Leith at the base of the Bernard Street triangle; it was sculpted by David Watson Stevenson in 1898. Several Edinburgh streets commemorate Burns — Robert Burns Drive in Liberton, Alloway Loan, Clarinda Terrace, Jean Armour Avenue, Mossgiel Walk and Shanter Way.

A calendar event all over Scotland and for all Caledonian Societies the world over is the celebration of Burns's birthday on the 25th January with a Burns Supper. He was born, the eldest of seven children, on the farm in Alloway in Ayrshire in the year 1759. Thomas Carlisle wrote in his Essays: 'Burns was born poor; and born also to continue poor, for he would not endeavour to be otherwise'. His hard-working father, William, insisted that his son's education was sound; young Robert devoured his studies. His mother, Agnes Burnes, undoubtedly influenced him and although she was barely literate she handed down to Robert a great amount of oral tradition. She loved to sing old Scots songs from her seemingly endless repertoire. Robert's imagination was fired with the stories of old Betty Davidson, a distant relative, who lived with the family and helped his mother. Burns wrote that 'she had the largest collection in the county of tales and songs concerning devils, ghosts, fairies, brownies, witches, warlocks, spunkies, kelpies, elf-candles, deil-lights, wraiths, apparitions, cantraips, giants, inchanted towers, dragons and other trumpery'. No doubt all of this helped to inspire *Tam O' Shanter* written many years later when Burns was an exciseman in Dumfries.

At Whitsun 1766 the family moved to another farm at Mount Oliphant, two miles from Alloway. William borrowed one hundred pounds to stock the farm. This was a hard and lonely time for the Burns family; the land was barren, mostly clay, and the loan became a heavy burden — but there were books aplenty in the Burns household and Robert read avariciously.

When Robert was fifteen he wrote his first love song to Helen Blair who worked beside him at harvest.

> *O once I love'd a bonnie lass*
> *An' aye I love her still*
> *An' whilst that virtue warms my breast*
> *I'll love my handsome Nell.*

The farm at Mount Oliphant almost ruined William Burnes. He and his wife and seven children moved to Lochlea between Tarbolton and Mauchline. Robert was nineteen when he began to socialise in Tarbolton and, to the annoyance of his Calvinist father, he learned to dance and to enjoy himself with his friends, David Sillar *(Epistle to Davie)*, John Rankine and John Wilson among them. With several others they formed the Bachelor's Club in which Burns, with his tendency to exhibitionism, led many debates. His comic song, *The Tarbolton Lassies*, gives a hint of his happy, carefree days with the lassies, but not with Elizabeth Gebbie (also known as Alison Begbie) who inspired three poems and the love song *Mary Morison*. She rejected his advances.

In the Freemasons of Tarbolton he rose to be Depute Master and, along with his brother Gilbert, experimented with flax-spinning at Lochlea. He move to Irvine in 1781 to progress this, but it ended in abject failure. There he met Richard Brown, a seaman, whose influence was great and who encouraged Burns not only to publish his poems but 'to endeavour at the character of a Poet'.

When his father died in 1784 Robert became the tenant farmer at Mossgiel. He first fathered a child by Elizabeth Paton and then fell deeply in love with his future wife, a 'Mauchline Belle', Jean Armour. At first, even though she was expecting his child, she changed her mind about marrying him — being pressurised against him by her father who despised Burns. Burns wrote to the Glasgow shoemaker David Brice of her: 'Never man loved, or rather adored, a woman more than I did her; and to confess a truth between you and me, I do still love her to distraction'.

He was sick of the drudgery of farming and having obtained a post in Jamaica he arranged to emigrate with Margaret Campbell, (Highland Mary). It was said that she died carrying Burns' child and he was deeply affected. On the 31st July 1786, in order to raise money, he published his first book, *Poems Chiefly in the Scottish Dialect* — this was the famous Kilmarnock edition, published by the Kilmarnock bookseller, John Wilson which brought immediate success and £20 for the 618 copies which were quickly snapped up. But he could still not afford the fare to Jamaica and it was Dr Blacklock, the blind minister from Edinburgh, who wrote to Burns and convinced him not to emigrate but to come to Edinburgh instead; luckily for posterity he heeded his advice.

On 3rd September Jean gave birth to twins which resolved Robert's mind to stay in Scotland. He had also chosen his poems carefully in order to avoid giving offence to the literary establishment which was to embrace him. He had taught himself to play the violin and displayed an acute ear for music; his use of the pentatonic scale to control tempo to suit his songs led to their perfection.

He was wined and dined by the high society of Edinburgh and, with his magnetic personality, his silvery tongue and his huge command of language, he more than held his own amongst the titled and the intelligensia. In the midst of all this euphoria Burns remained unaffected; he was more concerned about marrying Jean Armour whose father had by now warmed to the poet's apparent growing wealth

Burns's printer refused to undertake his second edition until he paid £27 for the paper, this was the Edinburgh edition of 1787. During his second visit to Edinburgh he temporarily forgot Jean Armour when, on 6th December 1787, he met Mrs McLehose — the beautiful, fascinating and intelligent poetess. Burns fell in love at first sight with his 'Clarinda' and she with her

'Sylvander'. His pen flowed with inspired love in *Clarinda, Mistress of my Soul* and in a stream of the most famous love letters ever written. An ardent lover, though he was, she kept him at arm's length and he returned to Mossgiel in 1788 to marry Jean Armour who had had another set of twins fated to die when only a few weeks old. The parting from Mrs McLehose was sad and sorrowful and he sent her *Ae Fond Kiss*, his most beautiful and heart-rending song.

He then moved in June 1788 to the tenancy of Ellisland Farm near Dumfries leaving Jean and the children at Mossgiel until a new farmhouse could be built. The farm was a poor living and by October 1789 he secured the post of Excise Officer at £50 per annum (a post obtained for him through the influence of the Earl of Glencairn) while Jean milked the cows and made butter and cheese. He was welcomed in Nithsdale where he became involved in politics, music, the formation of the parish library and theatre. His family life was settled and happy and Jean took in and cared for another of his illegitimate children, a daughter by Ann Park. Uncomplaining she looked after the baby girl with her own newly born baby boy. Burns was a competent exciseman and received two promotions and, with an increase in his annual salary to £70 plus perquisites and commission for seizures and fines, his annual total was about £150 (which equates to about £18,000 today).

Burns owed much to his friend and benefactor, the 14th Earl of Glencairn and when the Earl died in January 1791, Burns expressed his sorrow and gratitude in a short poem.

> *The Bridegroom may forget the Bride*
> *Was made his wedded wife Yestreen;*
> *The Monarch may forget the Crown*
> *That on his head an hour has been*
> *The Mother may forget the Child*
> *That smiles so sweetly on her knee;*
> *But I'll remember thee, Glencairn,*
> *And all that thou hast done for me!*
> *For all I have and all I am I owe to thee!*

In 1791 his landlord sold up Ellisland and the family moved into Dumfries. He was, somewhat to his annoyance, entertained, fêted and taken over by the gentry. His disgruntlement led to the occasional indiscretion but his open generosity of heart more than compensated. It was during this period that he met Maria Riddell, a young, intelligent and beautiful lady very much attracted to Burns but who refused his apology after one of his inebrious outbursts.

George Thomson, an Edinburgh clerk, wrote to Burns in September 1792 to ask for his help in improving the poetry of the melodies of Scotland for his publication, *A Select Collection of Original Scottish Airs for the Voice*. Burns replied with alacrity and enthusiasm. He refused payment with the words, 'You may think my songs above or below price, for they shall absolutely be one or the other. In honest enthusiasm with which I would embark on your undertaking, to talk of money, wages, fee, hire etc., would be downright sodomy of the soul!' *Scots Wha Hae* and *Auld Lang Syne* were written for this but the latter was published after Burns died.

In September of 1795 his daughter died; he was grief stricken and more so because he could not attend the funeral. He became increasingly ill and, on his doctor's advice, he waded into the sea each day at Brow Well on the Solway— a 'cure' which inevitably contributed to his death. In a letter to George Thomson dated April 1796 he wrote, 'I have only known existence by the pressure of the heavy hand of sickness; and have counted time by the repercussions of pain! Rheumatism, cold, fever, have formed to me a terrible combination. I close my eyes in misery and open them without hope.' He was not only ill but heavily in debt and worried to distraction. Only nine days before he died he wrote, again to Thomson, 'After all my boasted independence, curst the necessity compels me to implore you for five pounds … I do not ask all this gratuitously; for, upon returning health, I hereby promise and engage to furnish you with five pounds' worth of the neatest song-genius you have seen.' Thomson, friend that he was, sent a draft for the money and even thanked Burns for his request. Maria Riddell saw him shortly before he returned to Dumfries but Burns did not recover; he died in the early hours of 21st July 1796 aged only thirty-seven years. He was buried in St Michael's Churchyard in Dumfries. All Scotland mourned.

4 Royal Terrace

Leaving Calton Hill we arrive in the north-facing Royal
Terrace. This is a splendid design by William H. Playfair
whose revised drawings are dated 1824. Royal Terrace
overlooks Royal Terrace Gardens and its three sets of
seven, ten and another seven giant Corinthian
collonades have balustrades between them all with
arched entrances and ground-floor windows.

Royal Terrace was named to commemorate the
Royal visit to Edinburgh of George IV in 1822. This
was a great occasion; it was the first royal visit of a reigning monarch since that of Charles II in 1650. People
poured into Edinburgh from all over Scotland. The
King arrived at Leith on 14th August amid pouring
rain which did not prevent Sir Walter Scott from visiting him by rowing over to the Royal George. Scott had
been given the task of making the arrangements for
the royal visit and was warmly welcomed with, 'Sir
Walter Scott! The man in Scotland I most wish to see.
Let him come up.' Scott, overjoyed, presented the King
with a silver cross of St Andrew on behalf of the ladies
of Edinburgh.

Next day the royal procession travelled up Leith
Walk, along Waterloo Place, Regent Bridge and Regent Road (named after him when he was Prince Regent) to the Palace of Holyroodhouse. For the duration
of his stay in Scotland he resided at the Duke of
Buccleuch's house in Dalkeith and he visited Melville
Castle to review the Midlothian Cavalry and be entertained by Lord Melville

All his faults were forgotten and forgiven when he
displayed himself in the Stuart tartan which, according to Scott's son-in-law J.G. Lockhart in his *Life of Sir
Walter Scott*, started the cult of the tartan. George IV's
one redeeming feature was his ability to rise to the great
occasion; this was a never-to-be-forgotten spectacle.
Lockhart described it:

> Scott was determined to present the High-
> land chiefs in their traditional kilted glory,
> and to have as many other Scots as possi-
> ble (and also, on one occasion, the King
> himself) arrayed in tartan. This was his way
> of showing that George IV was now eve-

rywhere recognised as the legitimate successor to the old Stuart Kings of Scotland.

On the 22nd August his procession from Holyroodhouse, up the Royal Mile to the Castle was given a tumultuous reception and on the 23rd he reviewed the troops on Portobello sands (King's Road and Windsor Terrace and Place in Portobello were named to commemorate the occasion). Then he attended a magnificent banquet given in his honour by the peers of Scotland during which he conferred a baronetcy on the Lord Provost, William Arbuthnot. On the 29th he was entertained by the 4th Earl of Hopetoun at Hopetoun House where he knighted the famous Scottish portrait painter, Henry Raeburn. From there he left for Port Edgar where he departed by sea to London. (A biography of George IV is given in Capital Walk 1, number 21 on page 74.)

5   *Leopold Place*

Downhill from Calton Hill into Royal Terrace, the street opposite (looking across the gardens) is Leopold Place. It is part of London Road at the Leith Walk end and was designed as part of William H. Playfair's Calton scheme in 1820 with its magnificent Doric quadrant at the Elm Row end and its Ionic columns at the Windsor Street end. From its recently restored magnificence one can see why the Calton scheme might even have outshone the New Town had it been completed to Playfair's design.

It is named after Prince Leopold of Saxe-Coburg who was Queen Victoria's uncle and was invited to be King of Belgium in 1831. Belgium and Holland formed one kingdom at that time. The Belgians having fought the Dutch, driven them out and formed their own country, were looking for a king. The Prince had declined the throne of Greece and accepted Belgium instead. He visited Edinburgh on several occasions as the guest of Lord Provost Mackenzie. In 1817, he dined with him at his house in Gayfield Square and in 1819 he opened the Regent Bridge in Waterloo Place.

Leopold was born in Coburg, Germany on 16th December 1790, youngest son of Francis Frederick, Duke of Saxe-Coburg-Saalfeld. After a military education he served as a page at the court of Napoleon I and was commissioned in the Russian army. He became a general in 1813 and, fighting for the Russians, he was defeated at Lutzen and Bautzen near Dresden in Germany against the victorious Napoleon Bonaparte; however he gained victory at Leipzig in 1813. After the Duke of Wellington's victory at Waterloo and the final defeat of Napoleon, Leopold settled in Britain. In 1816 he married Charlotte, the only child of the disastrous marriage of George IV and Queen Caroline. Leopold's father-in-law, who was Prince Regent at the time of the marriage, detested the House of Coburg blaming this dynasty rather than himself for his own unhappy marriage to Princess Caroline. The young couple were popular and cheered wherever they went in England and this aggravated the Prince Regent. There were high hopes of an heir to the throne because it was common knowledge that the Prince Regent refused to live with his wife. Tragically, Charlotte died giving birth to a stillborn boy a year after her marriage to Leopold.

In 1829 Leopold married again — to a commoner, Caroline Bauer, but this morganatic marriage ended unhappily. Three years later he married Louise, daughter of Louise-Philippe, the citizen King of the French. They had three children: Leopold, Philip and Charlotte.

Leopold was elected King of the Belgians on 4th June 1831 and took the oath to the newly formed Belgian nation on 21st July 1831. He had Prime Minister Palmerston to thank for ensuring that Belgium was not partitioned as the French would have wished. In 1839 King Leopold successfully negotiated a treaty giving Belgium neutral status in the event of war in Europe; in international relations he achieved marked success but at home he preferred the old autocratic style of rule and attempted to link the clericals and Liberals to control Parliament. This failed and by 1847 he had no option but to recognise government by parties.

Through his many relations he became known as the 'Uncle of Europe', the marriage of his niece, Queen Victoria and his nephew, Prince Albert was brought about through his influence. He had arranged a short holiday for Albert and his brother Ernest to their cousin at Windsor. Victoria was entranced by the handsome Albert and they married three months later, on 10th February 1840. Prince Albert had been well taught by his uncle Leopold on the importance of monarchical government and Albert, in turn, taught the Queen about his place as her 'permanent minister', a position never recognised by Parliament.

Leopold's reign over the Belgians for thirty-four

years was one of wisdom and stability in which he skil-fully avoided revolution which had threatened almost all Europe. He died at Lacken on 10th December 1865 and was genuinely mourned in Belguim and in Britain — most especially by Queen Victoria who was still grieving over Prince Albert's death four years before.

6   Blenheim Place

From Royal Terrace we continue into Blenheim Place which was designed in 1821 as part of W.H. Playfair's Calton scheme. It curves round into Leith Walk. The Ionic portico on its gable drops to single storey houses to allow the view to Calton Hill. It is named after the Duke of Marlborough's victory at the Battle of Blenheim on 13th August 1704. Blenheim, called Höchstadt by the French and Germans, lies about twenty miles north-west of Nürnberg.

Louis XIV had become so powerful, it was feared by most states and Princes on the continent that their religious and political freedoms would be denied them. The Austrian Hapsburgs, as elected emperors of the Holy Roman Empire of Germany, were suspicious; a second Catholic counter-revolution was thought likely; the French army and navy had been increased. Almost a quarter of a million persecuted French Huguenots had fled during the 1670s and early 80s and continued to flee with Louis XIV's revocation of the Edict of Nantes in 1685. He had swallowed up Strasbourg and the Alsace; Luxembourg was forced to recognise him and the might of his army increased its grip on Italy — all contributing to the Nine Years' War (1689-98) and the War of Spanish Succession (1702-13); it was in the latter that the Battle of Blenheim was a key victory.

The Franco-Bavarian armies, having retreated to Augsburg, were reinforced by French forces under their general, Compte Camille de Tallard and, while Prince Eugène of Savoy held the Rhine, Marlborough attacked the Bavarians. The Allies captured Donaüworth in a bloody battle to cross the river into Bavaria having, if required, a line of retreat to Nürnberg. Marlborough created a diversion by detaching Baden to attack Ingolstadt to the east and the French attacked Prince Eugène having re-crossed the river — a manoeuvre anticipated by Marlborough who had joined Prince Eugène on 10th August.

Imagining that the Allies would retreat to Nürnberg the French general, Compte Camille de Tallard, positioned his army in readiness to attack. Instead of retreating, Marlborough resplendent in his red uniform and riding a white horse, surprised the enemy in a dawn attack on the 13th August. The opposing armies, about equal in strength, formed a four-mile front. Eugène attacked the right wing and Lord John Cutts attacked the village of Blenheim; both were held by the French.

It was at this point that Marlborough saw the enemy's mistake; Tallard had concentrated his infantry in Blenheim and had failed to notice the Allies surreptitious crossing of the river Nebel during the previous night. Marlborough dug deep into the enemy's left centre, breaking it decisively; the French retreated to Ulm, broken and straggling. Tallard himself was taken prisoner, the French having lost 30,000 killed and wounded. The English, Dutch and Germans took thousands of prisoners and shared the French guns, money and food. Marlborough had a narrow escape from death when a cannonball struck the ground only inches from him.

He was the hero and victor of Blenheim; he pencilled a hurried note to his wife, Sarah: 'I have not time to say more but to beg you will give my duty to the Queen, and let her know her army has had a glorious victory. Monsieur Tallard and two other generals are in my coach and I am following the rest. The bearer, my aide-de-camp, Colonel Parke, will give her an account of what has passed. I shall do it in a day or two by another more large.' This short note, delivered one week after the greatest victory since the Middle Ages, was the first news to reach England.

Marlborough recrossed the Rhine and prepared for his great campaign to cross the Vosges and to take Trèves (now Trier) in Luxembourg. He had effectively ended Louis XIV's monarchy. He returned home to receive a Dukedom from Queen Anne with a present of the Royal manor of Woodstock and a promise of £240,000 to build Blenheim Palace.

7 Baxter's Place

Into Leith Walk, Baxter's Place is part of the main street. It is named after John Baxter, an architect who feued 'Baxter's Buildings' from the Town Council in 1780. He designed Mortonhall House at Frogston Road East for the Trotter family in 1769 and St Patrick's RC Church in the Cowgate, 1771-74 (originally built for rich Episcopalians). He died in 1798.

The home of Robert Stevenson, the engineer and grandfather of RL Stevenson

Robert Stevenson House, at Nos. 1-3 Baxter's Place, is now occupied by Longman Group UK Ltd. It was originally the offices of the engineer, Robert Stevenson, grandfather of RL Stevenson.

The Bell Rock lighthouse, in the estuary of the River Tay, is a monument to Robert Stevenson's fortitude, courage and genius. That infamous rock claimed hundreds of lives in shipping tragedies because of its invisibility to seamen. It was submerged by twelve feet of swirling seas at high tide and barely visible at low tide. In the terrible storm of 1799 alone, seventy vessels were wrecked on or near the rock.

Many had tried to erect a beacon on this terror-ridden rock and had failed. Stevenson surveyed it the year after the disasters and submitted his design and a model of a tower two days before Christmas of 1800. It took six years of patient persuasion and argument before Parliament passed the Bill to allow its erection after hearing evidence from the eminent Scottish civil engineer, John Rennie supported by Robert Stevenson. Rennie was appointed consulting engineer even though he was without experience in lighthouse building; he suggested several alterations to Stevenson's design which were accepted with alacrity. Stevenson's son, Alan, wrote in his *Memoir of Robert Stevenson, Civil Engineer* in 1861:

> To the very last the bankers were in doubt as to their security on the dues for so great and hazardous an undertaking; and the Bill included an authority to borrow £25,000 from the Exchequer.

Stevenson and his team of workers suffered unbelievable hardships for the next five years during its construction, and the beacon of that famous lighthouse shone for the first time on 1st February 1811. There has been no loss of life on the Bell Rock since.

Robert Stevenson was born on 8th June 1772 at Glasgow, the only child of Alan Stevenson who died in St Christopher (St Kitts) in the West Indies when Robert was two years old. His mother, Jean, re-married fourteen years later having suffered hard times during which Robert was educated at a Charity School. Her second husband, Thomas Smith, had been appointed engineer to the newly constituted Northern Lighthouse Board (1786) which still has its offices in No 84 George Street and is easily recognised from the model lighthouse above its entrance.

Although it was intended that Robert should enter the Church, he was employed in his stepfather's office and he took up his studies in civil engineering at the Andersonian Institute (now Strathclyde University) and completed them at the University of Edinburgh. He was excluded from graduating MA because, he explains. 'Of my slender knowledge of Latin in which my highest book was the Orations of Cicero, and by my total want of Greek.' He was given great encouragement by his stepfather who allowed him to superintend a number of lighthouse buildings and their macadam access roads; he worked on lanterns and optical equipment — all of which gave him excellent training and experience.

Such was his success that he was made a partner with his stepfather and that year, 1796, he married his stepsister, (Smith's daughter by a previous marriage). The young couple lived at No.1 Baxter's Place.

When Smith retired, Stevenson was appointed

engineer to the Scottish Lighthouse Board and proceeded energetically to design and construct twenty new lighthouses and to improve, through his ingenious designs, the reflecting (catoptric) and the refracting (dioptric) systems of lighting. He invented the intermittent or flashing light system for which the King of the Netherlands awarded him a gold medal.

During the construction of the Bell Rock lighthouse he introduced many new designs and inventions — for the first time in lighthouse construction the stone floors were 'bonded' to tie the walls together to prevent outward thrust; he introduced lightning protection (which Faraday advocated later for the Eddystone lighthouse). The total cost of the completed tower was £41,000.

Stevenson, the man, was described by Sir Walter Scott — 'a most gentlemanlike and modest man and well known by his scientific skill.' Stevenson did not confine himself to lighthouses however; he undertook many engineering projects with other famous engineers of the day, Rennie, Nimmo, Telford, Walker and Cubitt. The Hutchison Bridge, 'one of the best specimens of the segmental arch' was Stevenson's as was his new design of the suspension bridge with its roadway above; its chains avoided the need for tall piers. For railways Stevenson's design, using malleable iron for rails, was used later by George Stephenson; he emphasised the importance of accurately drawn charts from careful marine surveys by soundings. Nearer to home, Stevenson designed and executed the eastern road approaches to Edinburgh by the Calton Hill — London Road and Regent Road; he extended Princes Street to Waterloo Place. He was one of the originators of the Royal Observatory of Edinburgh, the engineer for the railway through West Princes Street Gardens and was consulted about the foundation for the Melville monument in St Andrew Square. He also built the breakwater at Newhaven.

He was elected to fellowship of the Royal Society of Edinburgh in 1815 and was a member of the Institution of Civil Engineers. He wrote for the *Edinburgh Encyclopaedia, the Encyclopaedia Britannica* and he contributed many papers to learned societies.

He died aged seventy-eight years at his house in Baxter's Place, not living to see his grandson, Robert Louis Stevenson, who was born only four months after his death on 12th July 1850. He is buried in the New Calton Cemetery.

The large college in the west of the city at Sighthill commemorates his name — Stevenson College of Further Education (of which the author was first Principal).

8   Union Place

Union Place is the street opposite Baxter's Place and was named to commemorate the Union of Ireland with Britain on 1st January 1801. Union Street, off Leith Walk, at Antigua Street was developed from 1800 as part of the Gayfield and Picardy estates.

Some historians describe the nineteen year period between 1782 and 1801 as the 'Irish Problem' but since 1650 restrictions and deprivations against Catholics had led to their abject poverty, utter misery and unbearable starvation with consequent loss of life. The Irish Parliament was bound up by British rule; standard British liberties did not exist in Ireland and markets were lost because of the American War which caused even greater poverty.

The Irish Volunteer movement of almost 80,000 demanded more freedom of trade and government. The concessions of 1780-83 rapidly opened up colonial trade bringing some prosperity, but the next six years were disastrous; the postponements of Union with Britain, Parliamentary reform and Catholic emancipation opened up old wounds.

The French Revolution encouraged the republican movement towards reform and independence. The Society of United Irishmen founded by a Protestant lawyer, Wolfe Tone, gained support from British democratic societies and from the French Convention. The Irish aristocratic Catholics petitioned George III in 1792; he believed that Catholic emancipation would violate the Coronation Oath. The Catholics conspired together and the Protestants formed their Orange Order in 1795. Ulstermen who had joined the yeomanry, terrorised Catholic communities and used their support of union with Britain to justify their cause.

The government felt it should support the Orangemen and in 1797 martial law, curfew and house burning led to anarchy; the rebellion of 1798 was hopeless from its start. Feargus O'Connor, the Irish Chartist, was caught on his way to France, the Leinster Committee was arrested and Lord Edward Fitzgerald was betrayed and killed in his attempt to organise a French invasion. It took 45,000 troops commanded by the Lord Lieutenant, Charles, 1st Marquis Cornwallis, to maintain order, but 12,000 rebels had been killed. The British cabinet accepted that Union was the only answer; the first attempt was defeated in 1799, the Protestants were against it but Pitt, Dundas, Cornwallis and Castlereagh argued for emancipation as a concomitant of the settlement. Progress for the Union was slow; most United Irishmen, the Catholic prelates and the Ulster linen merchants were in favour but the Orange Order was split. The Dublin parliament passed it in February 1800 and the Act received Royal assent in August. In the 'United Kingdom' Parliament, Ireland would have four Lords spiritual, twenty-eight Lords temporal and one hundred Commoners. The Cabinet discussed the admission of Catholics and Dissenters if they took an amended oath of allegiance. The King was furious, Cornwallis resigned, the Cabinet was split and George III accepted Pitt's resignation ending any hope of a just settlement. However, the King's insanity recurred in February and to pacify him Pitt agreed to drop emancipation and the Union was signed on 1st January 1801. It united the established Churches, allowed a united exchequer, established free trade and Pitt had given a tacit promise of emancipation. But the Union ultimately failed and the Irish Home Rule Movement brought about Irish Partition in 1920-22.

9 Picardy Place

Just round the corner from Union Street is Picardy Place which leads to York Place. It is now a single-sided street, its southern half having been demolished in 1969 to make space for a traffic island as a preliminary to the inner ring road which was never made. However on the new pedestrian area is the statue of Sherlock Holmes, the fictional character created by Sir Arthur Conan Doyle who was born on 22nd May 1859 in Picardy Place. The cost of the statue, designed by Gerald Laing, was shared by Edinburgh District Council and businessman Tom Farmer CBE of Kwik Fit.

THE STATUE OF CONAN DOYLE'S FAMOUS DETECTIVE IN PICARDY PLACE

Picardy Place derives its name from the district of Picardy in northern France from which the refugee Protestant Huguenots fled after Louis XIV revoked the Edict of Nantes in 1685. He had just married his mistress, the cold-hearted Madame de Maintenon. She, a Catholic, had been governed by Jesuits and after the revocation the Protestants were subjected to a long and bloody persecution. Over half a million of them fled the country and France lost many of its best artisans. The Huguenots were devotees of John Calvin, the Swiss reformer. The French Wars of Religion, 1562-98, caused the split between Catholics and Huguenots but the Edict of Nantes of 1598 allowed the two creeds to co-exist. Its revocation made Louis XIV hated by Protestants.

Five acres of land was feued from the Heriot Trust in 1730 for the Huguenot silk weaver colony. They tried to grow mulberry bushes on the ground sloping from the present St Andrew Square but did not succeed. The colony land, known as the Old Weavers Village or Little Picardy, was eventually taken over by the Commissioners for the Improvement of Manufacturers and in 1803 Robert Burn designed the three-storey tenements. The south side of Picardy Place was demolished but the north side with its long palace-front and its five-bay Ionic pilastered centre remains.

At No. 2 Picardy Place a brass plate is inscribed:

> Arthur Conan Doyle, creator of Sherlock Holmes, was born at number 11 opposite here on 22nd May 1859. This was a southern Irishman with all the beloved characteristics of his race, 'big-hearted, big-bodied, big-souled'.

His forebears were Irish country squires and as Catholics they fell victim to the Penal Laws with the loss of their estates and fortunes which were regained by Conan Doyle. But the family ruin appears to have released a latent creative energy. The Doyles form an illustrious family; within three generations, five of them (including Conan Doyle), appear in the *Dictionary of National Biography* having gained national distinction.

Conan Doyle was born in Edinburgh and educated at Stonyhurst and Edinburgh University where he graduated MD. He practised medicine in Southsea and in London and took up writing simply to supplement a meagre income. Conan Doyle's development in logic and deduction in the Edinburgh University class of 1876-81 is certainly due to the teaching of Dr Bell. The creation of Holmes and Watson and the powers of deductive observation endowed upon the fictional Holmes have made him seem a living person — the essence of brilliant authorship. Doyle's first publication was for *Chamber's Journal* in 1879. This was followed by his detective stories which were serialised by *The Strand Magazine* — *The Adventures of Sherlock Holmes*, between 1891-1893 and from which the books, *The Sign of Four* and *The Hound of the Baskervilles* were published.

Conan Doyle did more than simply write his stories, he gave practical assistance to the Police Forces in England; for example, he found a murderer who had led the Police to believe that he had disappeared and his body destroyed. He commented upon cases of mistaken identity; *Edaljee* in 1903 and *Oscar Slater* in 1909. He was involved in the training of police in Egypt; the French Sureté named their Crime Laboratory in Lyon in his honour; the Police College of China paid tribute to him. He advised on military, medical and even religious matters; he warned Berliners in 1890 that Professor Robert Koch's lymph-inoculation cure (tuberculin) was doubtful; his suggestion in a letter to *The Times* during the Boer War led to the creation of the Imperial Yeomanry. He served as an army doctor during the South African War (1899-1902) and after his publication of *The War in South Africa* in which he explained and justified the British action, he was knighted by Edward VII in 1902.

When Queen Victoria died he wrote to *The Times* advocating a change in the Coronation oath to effectively delete the insult to Catholics — this was done. He predicted the use of submarines by Germany long before the Great War and he advocated the concept of a Channel tunnel. He protested at the lack of lifebelts on warships and was said to have been the father of the Home Guard. But he puzzled many of his devotees by his conversion to spiritualism, a subject on which he wrote towards the end of his life.

Conan Doyle himself considered *The Man from Archangel* from his *Tales of Adventure* to be his finest piece of writing. For his preparation before writing the historical romance, *The White Company* he isolated himself for a year in a small cottage in the New Forest with sixty-five works of reference on every aspect of the 14th century. Other books of great literary merit included *Micah Clarke, Brigadier Gerard, Sir Nigel* and *Rodney Stone*. He took up oil painting only a year before his death in 1930 having written over 70 books.

10 York Place

York Place is the con-
tinuation of Picardy
Place and leads to
Queen Street. It was
originally part of Queen
Street in James Craig's
plan of the New Town
and its first feues were
bought in 1793 after the
land had been bought
from James Erskine,
Lord Alva. No.47 York
Place was the birthplace
of James Nasmyth
(1808-90) the inventor of
the steam hammer and
at No.32 Sir Henry
Raeburn built a studio
and a large portrait gallery.

*NO 32 YORK PLACE, HOME
OF SIR HENRY RAEBURN*

York Place is named after George III's second son,
the Duke of York, whose Scottish title is the Duke of
Albany, from which Albany Street (parallel to and north
of York Place) is named. His biography is in Capital
Walk 1, number 3 on page 24.

Sir Henry Raeburn (1756-1823) was the Scottish
portrait painter and pioneer of direct painting in which
he painted direct on to the canvas without preparatory
drawings. Henry Raeburn was born in Stockbridge on
4th March 1756, the younger of two sons. He was six
years old when his father, a yarn-boiler, died and he
was cared for by his elder brother, William. He attended
George Heriot's School where his caricatures of the
teachers were a source of great hilarity. He left Heriot's
aged sixteen to be apprenticed to a goldsmith, James
Gilliland, in Parliament Close. It was during this time
that his copies of miniatures were much admired and
by the age of twenty, and self-taught except for some
lessons from his employer's friend, David Deuchar, he
was already in demand for his larger portraits. Within
eight years he had become the leading portrait painter
in Scotland.

While painting a landscape, Ann Edgar, widow of
Count Leslie, (after whom Leslie Place is named) ad-

SIR HENRY RAEBURN (1756-1823)

mired his work and called at his studio to have her portrait painted. He was captivated by her; they fell in love and were married in 1780. They made their home at Deanhaugh House (now demolished) in Stockbridge. He, aged twenty-four and she thirty-six with three children, adored each other; their marriage was perfectly happy. Secluded, tranquil Ann Street is named after her; it was planned in 1814 and credited to architect James Milne.

Encouraged by Sir Joshua Reynolds, painter to George III, the happy couple spent two years in Italy. Just before he left, Sir Joshua, concerned for their welfare, whispered to young Henry: 'Young man, I know nothing of your circumstances. Young painters are seldom rich; but if money be necessary for your studies abroad, say so, and you shall not want.' Raeburn was touched and grateful to have letters of introduction but he declined the generous offer of money.

After his return to Scotland in 1787 he was in such demand that he could choose not only those who wanted their portraits painted but, more importantly to him, the character of the painting. With this success and his inherited wealth he built a large gallery at No.32 York Place in 1798 to continue his success which was marred only by his son's bankruptcy in 1808. This led to his own bankruptcy and he had to sell his York Place studio. Two years later his affairs were settled.

He was elected President of the Society of Arts in Edinburgh in 1812, and made a full Academician of the Royal Academy in London where he had exhibited in 1792 having been elevated from membership to full academician. Of his election he wrote:

> I observe what you say respecting the election of an RA; but what am I to do here? They know that I am on their list; if they choose to elect me without solicitation, it will be the more honourable to me, and I will think the more of it; but if it can only be obtained by means of solicitation and canvassing I must give up all hopes of it, for I would think it unfair to employ those means.

Raeburn was knighted at Hopetoun House in 1822 when George IV was the guest of the 4th Earl of Hopetoun and he was made His Majesty's Limner for Scotland just before he died. Some twenty-six of his portraits may be viewed in the National Museum of Antiquities and Portrait Gallery of Scotland in Queen Street.

11 Elder Street

Elder Street, off York Place, leads to the Bus Station, St James Centre and New St Andrews House; little is left of the original street which was named after Thomas Elder, a successful merchant of Edinburgh who was elected to the Town Council in 1770. He was elected to the office of Lord Provost three times — the first to exceed two terms of office since George Drummond who held the Lord Provostship six times.

Thomas Elder was born in 1737, the eldest son of William Elder of Loaning and Elizabeth Man. He was a successful wine merchant and was elected a Town Councillor in 1770. In 1765 he married Emilia, eldest daughter of Paul Husband of Logie; they had one son and four daughters.

After eighteen years of intermittent service to the Town Council, his election as Lord Provost for the first time was in 1788. His second term of office coincided with the French Revolution and he was very much involved with the suppression of any who were sympathetic towards its aims. He actively suppressed meetings of the 'Friends of the People' and he took personal responsibility in breaking up a meeting of the British Convention on 5th December 1793 when he imprisoned ten of its leaders. The Town Council presented him with an embellished plate for 'his spirited and prudent conduct while in office and especially during the late commotions'.

Elder was a close friend of Henry Dundas of

Arniston, Lord Melville, and Prime Minister William Pitt. Civil war, especially in Scotland where economic suffering was worst, was a genuine fear and Elder was the first Colonel of the Royal Edinburgh Volunteers.

The French had declared war on Britain and Holland on 31st January 1793 and during Elder's third term of office as Lord Provost, from 1796 to 1798, he entertained the exiled Compte d'Artois, grandson of Louis XV, who became Charles X of France and who was driven into exile in 1830. Elder organised a subscription for £1,000 towards the war against the French.

Elder's interest in the university, or 'tounis college', as it was known at that time, was evident from the pressure he exerted to have it rebuilt; its foundation stone was laid by Lord Napier of Merchiston on 16th November 1789 during Elder's first Provostship. Elder's influence was such that he was able to ensure the success of his son-in-law, George Baird, in his election to the Principalship of the college in succession to Principal Robertson. The Principal and his professors commissioned Sir Henry Raeburn to paint Elder's portrait in 1797; it was hung in the Court room of the college. Thomas Elder's last office was that of Postmaster General of Scotland; he died on 29th May 1799 aged sixty-two at the village of Forneth near Blairgowrie, four years after his appointment.

12 St James Centre

St James Centre was designed by Burke, Martin and partners in 1964. This large concrete shopping centre was greatly enhanced by the John Lewis extension in 1990. It remains, however, an architectural incongruity in the capital.

The tenements and shops which replaced the original St James's Square were first feued in 1773 and designed by James Craig. The tenements of St James's Square were demolished to make way for the present modern concrete structure — St James Centre.

St James Square, its adjoining streets and Little King Street, which was situated on the south side of St Mary's Cathedral, were said to have been named after the 'Old Pretender' who, had his rebellion succeeded, would have become James VIII of Scotland, III of England. After the failure of the 1715 rebellion the Jacobites were cautious and hid his name under the title 'St James'. However Little King Street, which ran downhill from the Square past St Mary's Cathedral, openly commemorated James Francis Edward Stuart, Prince of Wales, Chevalier de St George, the 'Old Pretender'.

Scotland and England had had enough of the Stuarts and after James VII of Scotland (II of England) was deposed he was replaced by William of Orange and Princess Mary (James's daughter) who were crowned following their acceptance, on 13th February 1689, of the Declaration of Rights in England and the Claim of Rights in Scotland to ensure that the abuses of James VII were never repeated.

When James VII died in 1701 his son, aged thirteen, became the 'Pretender' to the throne. The main objection to him was his religion; he was a resolute Catholic and a return to 'absolutism' was dreaded — but not by his Jacobite supporters in England and Scotland who dreamed of the return of the Stuarts to the throne.

James Francis Edward Stuart was born on 10th June 1688 in St James's Palace, the only son of James VII (II of England) by his second wife, Mary of Modena. Even on the announcement of his birth there was suspicion of deception; it seemed too much of a coincidence to produce a son almost at the time of his dethronement. For his safety the baby prince was sent to a fortress in Portsmouth while his father set out for Salisbury to tackle William of Orange. When James II had to flee the young prince was taken to France with his mother. In 1701 as James II lay dying, Louis XIV promised that the child would be acknowledged King of England. He kept his promise when the king died and, in Paris, he heralded the boy as James III of England and VIII of Scotland.

The Act of Settlement of 21st June 1701 excluded the male line of the Stuarts from succession and Queen Anne, when she succeeded the throne in 1702, showed no favour to her half-brother. His letter requesting recognition as her heir was ignored.

In Scotland Lord Lovat tried the 'Scots Plot' in 1704 but it was a miserable failure. However Lieutenant Nathaniel Hooke, reporting to Louis XIV, recommended that there was sufficient support for a Jacobite rising and after equipping ships and 4,000 troops the young prince was launched into battle with the words: 'The best wish I can make you is that I may never see your face again'. However the whole lot turned back when they spied the English fleet under Admiral Byng.

Back in France the Chevalier fought against the English in Flanders, but after Louis XIV's monarchy was destroyed and the Treaty of Utrecht signed (1713) with provision for the removal of the Chevalier from the Dominions of France, he had to seek refuge in Italy. When Queen Anne died and George I was proclaimed king in Edinburgh on 5th August 1714 the Jacobites, who had hoped that the 'Pretender' would be restored, were bitterly disappointed. They started to re-arm and on the 7th of September the Earl of Mar raised the standard at Castleton in Braemar. On the government side the Duke of Argyll was chosen. Mar procrastinated and on the day that the Jacobites were beaten at Preston, Mar and Argyll met at Sheriffmuir. It was a strange battle, no one could decide who had won:

It seems that the Chevalier had been told of victory and he landed in disguise at Peterhead on 22nd December. He was joined by Mar and a small army at Perth where he was openly proclaimed King James VIII of Scotland, III of England. On 2nd January 1716 he journeyed to Brechin, Glamis and Dundee where he made a state entry to be given a warm welcome. At Scone preparations were made for his coronation, Jacobite ladies having given their jewels for his crown, but his presence was uninspiring; he seemed weak and easily manipulated by self-seeking nobles. In contrast the Highland chiefs showed their readiness to fight but the Chevalier quickly departed across the ice of the River Tay to Montrose when word came of the approach of Argyll's army.

From France he wrote two letters: one to the Duke of Argyll enclosing money to be distributed among the sufferers and the other to General Gordon thanking his followers for their devotion and explaining that he had deserted them for their own good.

The death of Charles II of Sweden ended the Chevalier's hopes of a Swedish-Jacobite invasion but the King of Spain agreed to equip an expedition of 5,000 men with arms for 3,000 more to link up with the Earl Marischal's subsidiary force. It surrendered at the Pass of Glenshiels on 1st April 1719, the Spanish having been driven back by a storm. Meanwhile the Chevalier had remained at a safe distance in Madrid where he married Princess Maria Clementina, the grandaughter of the King of Poland. He then retired to Rome. In 1722 another expedition foundered due to lack of money and support. His wife left him and he, dispirited and depressed, took to drink; his supporters turned their affections to his son, Charles Edward.

The Chevalier, still had thoughts of the English throne and he freely gave up his Papal pension to fit out another expedition — the '45 Rebellion. Charles Edward promised to 'lay three crowns at his feet', but his rather weak reply was: 'Be careful, my dear boy, for I would not lose you for all the crowns in the world'. The '45 caught the imagination of all Jacobites; the handsome, twenty-five year old 'Bonnie Prince Charlie' raised the Standard for the last time at Glenfinnan on the 19th August 1745 and after successive victories he marched his army the three hundred miles to Derby, just over one hundred miles from his goal — London. His Highland Chieftains were sick of marching and fighting; they quarrelled among themselves and they decided to abandon the great cause. Charles was dejected and his army was in no fit state to meet the fresh, well trained 9,000 strong army of the Duke of Cumberland (brother of George II). The Jacobite army of 5,000 tired men were slaughtered by 'Butcher

Cumberland' at Culloden Moor on the 16th April 1746. Charles escaped to France and Italy in spite of the £30,000 reward for his head.

In 1756 the Pope issued an order that all his subjects should style the Chevalier, King of England but the Italians had little respect for him. It was said of him that 'he never affected the least power, he seemed totally indifferent to all affairs, both of a public and a domestic nature'. He died in the evening of 1st January 1766 and was buried in the Church of St Peter's in Rome where a monument by Canova was erected in 1819 at the expense of George III. His son, the Young Pretender, retired to Florence and assumed the title Charles III and died in Rome 22 years after his father in 1788.

References

1. History and Derivation of Edinburgh Street Names, by Edinburgh Corporation City Engineers Department, 1975.
2. The Streets of Edinburgh, various authors. Pub. Edinburgh Impressions.
3. Essential Edinburgh by Alan Hamilton. Pub. Andre Deutch Ltd.
4. Dictionary of National Biography, Ed Leslie Stephen and Syndey Lee. Pub Smith Elder & Co. Ltd.
5. The Oxford Dictionary of Saints, New Edition by David Hugh Farmer. Pub. Oxford University Press.
6. Chambers Biographical Dictionary, Ed. J.O.Thorne MA, T.C.Collocott MA. Pub. W & R Chambers Ltd.
7. The Lives of the Kings and Queens of England, Ed. Antonia Fraser. Pub. MacDonald Futura Publishers.
8. Scottish Kings, by Gordon Donaldson. Pub. Book Club Associates, London.
9. Late Great Britons, Pub. Brook Productions for the BBC.
10. Who's Who in Scottish History, by Gordon Donaldson and Robert 5. Morpeth, Pub. Basil Blackwell, Oxford.
11. Memorials of his Time, by Lord Cockburn, Pub. Robert Grant & Son Ltd.
12. Old and New Edinburgh, vols. I-TIT by James Grant, Pub. Cassell & Co. Ltd.
13. A Hotbed of Genius, The Scottish Enlightenment, 1730-90, Ed. Daiches, Jones & Jones, Pub. Edinburgh University Press.
14. Edinburgh, by David Daiches, Pub. Granada Publishing Ltd.
15. Georgian Edinburgh, by Ian G. Lindsay, revised

by David Walker, Pub. Scottish Academic Press.

16. The Buildings of Scotland: Edinburgh, by John Gifford, Colin McWilliam and David Walker, Pub. Penguin Books.

17. Scotland's Story in Her Monuments, by David GrahamCampbell, Pub. Robert Hale, London.

18. A History of England, by Keith Feiling, Pub. Book Club Associates.

19. The Story of a Nation, Scotland, A Concise History, by P. Hume Brown revised by H.W. Meikle, Pub. Lang Syne Publishers Ltd.

20. Scotland, A New History, by Michael Lynch, Pub. Century Ltd.

21. Traditions of Edinburgh, by Robert Chambers LL.D., Pub. W&R Chambers Ltd.

22. Edinburgh, The Third Statistical Account of Scotland: The City of Edinburgh, Ed. David Keir, Pub. Collins Glasgow.

23. Edinburgh in the Nineteenth Century, by Thomas H. Shepherd and John Britton, Pub. Arno Press, New York.

24. Famous Scots, The Pride of a Small Nation, by Forbes MacGregor, Pub. Gordon Wright Publishing, Edinburgh.

25. The Romance of the Edinburgh Streets, by Mary D. Steuart, Pub. Methuen & Co. Ltd.

26. Scottish portrait, by Augustus Muir, Pub. The Hoptoun Press, Edinburgh.

27. A Small Country, by Neil McCallum, Pub. James Thin, The Mercat Press.

28. Book of the Old Edinburgh Club, Vol XXVIII, Printed by T & A Constable.

29. Great Men of Scotland, by Theo Land, Pub. The Bodley Head.

30. 101 Great Scots, by Allan Massie, Pub. W & R Chambers Ltd.

31. Edinburgh Portraits, by Michael Turnbull, Pub. John Donald Publishers Ltd.

32. The Lord Provosts of Edinburgh 1296-1932, by Marguerite Wood, Pub. T & A Constable at The University Press.

33. I Can Remember Robert Louis Stevenson, Ed. Rosaline Masson, Pub. W & R Chambers Ltd.

34. Robert Louis Stevenson, by Lord Guthrie, Pub. W. Green & Son Ltd., Edinburgh.

35. Wellington, The Years of the Sword, by Elizabeth Longford, Pub. World Books, London.

36. Lord Provost George Drummond 1687-1766, by various authors, Pu. Scotland's Cultural Heritage, University of Edinburgh, 1987.

37. Abridged Statistical History of Scotland, by James Hooper Dawson, Pub. W & H Lizars, London and Samuel Highley & Son, 1853.

38. Anecdotes and Facts of Scotland and Scotsmen, by James Mitchell LL.D, Printed for J.Anderson, jun.,Edinburgh, J. Cumming, Dublin and Sherwood Jones & Co., London. 1825.

39. The Making of Classical Edinburgh, by A.J. Youngson, Pub. Edinburgh University Press.

40. Nelson, by Carola Oman, Pub. The Reprint Society, London.

41. Edinburgh 1329-1929, Pub. Oliver & Boyd, Edinburgh, 1929.

42. Civic Survey & Plan for Edinburgh, prepared for the Town Council by Patrick Abercrombie LL.D and Derek Plumstead, ARIBA. Pub. Oliver & Boyd, Edinburgh, 1949.